THE
POISON
EATERS

FIGHTING DANGER AND FRAUD IN OUR FOOD AND DRUGS

BY
GAIL JARROW

CALKINS CREEK
AN IMPRINT OF BOYDS MILLS & KANE
New York

For information about permission to reproduce selections from this book, please contact permissions@bmkbooks.com.

Calkins Creek
An Imprint of Boyds Mills & Kane
calkinscreekbooks.com
Printed in China

ISBN: 978-1-62979-438-9 (hardcover)
ISBN: 978-1-68437-895-1 (eBook)

Library of Congress Control Number: 2019936023
First edition

10 9 8 7 6 5 4 3 2 1

Designed by Red Herring Design
Titles set in Brandon Printed and ITC Barcelona
Text set in ITC Century

CONTENTS

8 CHAPTER ONE
EMBALMED BEES *and* OTHER DELICACIES

13 CHAPTER TWO
FARM BOY

21 CHAPTER THREE
CHEMICAL FEAST

36 CHAPTER FOUR
The POISON EATERS

54 CHAPTER FIVE
MORPHINE, MEAT, *and* MUCKRAKERS

70 CHAPTER SIX
"JANITOR *of the* PEOPLE'S INSIDES"

86 CHAPTER SEVEN
OLD BORAX

93 CHAPTER EIGHT
RADIOACTIVE MIRACLES

105 CHAPTER NINE
RASPBERRY COUGH SYRUP

114 CHAPTER TEN
The WATCHDOGS

124 THE POISON SQUAD CHEMICALS

126 GLOSSARY

128 TIMELINE

131 MORE TO EXPLORE

134 AUTHOR'S NOTE

136 SOURCE NOTES

144 BIBLIOGRAPHY

149 INDEX

153 PICTURE CREDITS

An illustration from *Puck* magazine, October 1900, shows a pharmacist at The Kill Em' Quick Pharmacy selling dangerous drugs to eager customers . . . including children. Bottles of opium, cocaine, strychnine, and soothing syrup tempt buyers.

For Robert

ACKNOWLEDGMENTS

Thank you to the following people for their generous help with my research—historical, chemical, governmental, and photographic: Alyssa Constad, General Federation of Women's Clubs; Professor R. Bertrum Diemer Jr., Chemical and Biomolecular Engineering, University of Delaware; Dr. Suzanne Junod, Historian, U.S. Food and Drug Administration; Rochelle Proujansky; Professor Joe M. Regenstein, Department of Food Science, Cornell University; Dean Rogers, Special Collections Library, Vassar College; and the staffs of the Library of Congress Manuscript Reading Room and Prints and Photographs Reading Room.

As always, I sing the praises of the meticulous and creative team at Calkins Creek, most of all my gifted editor, Carolyn P. Yoder.

—G.J.

An early-twentieth-century advertisement shows that borax was used as laundry soap. It was also used as a food preservative.

CHAPTER ONE

EMBALMED BEES and OTHER DELICACIES

"There is Death in the pot."
—Chemist Fredrick Accum, quoting *2 Kings 4:40*

You're so hungry you don't have to be called twice for dinner.

It's 1890, and you live in a large town or city, just like a third of Americans. Your grandparents had a farm and grew their own food. Now, your mother and all her friends buy food at a grocery store.

You pick up your fork and dig in. The meat on your plate was supposed to be chicken, but it sure doesn't look or smell like that. Actually, it's cheap, fatty pork someone a thousand miles away stuffed in a can and shipped to your neighborhood store.

The sausage sizzling in the pan also came from a filthy factory a thousand miles away. It was made from a pulverized mass of meat scraps swept off the floor—along with the rat feces—and mixed with borax to keep it from rotting.

[Borax is the same stuff in scouring powder and laundry detergent.]

The peas are bright green and look delicious. The company that canned them added copper sulfate to enhance the color.

[Today this chemical is used to prevent wood rot and pond scum.]

The milk in the bottle was watered down. Then a dash of formaldehyde was stirred in to keep it fresh longer.

[Formaldehyde is used to embalm dead bodies . . . and not recommended for drinking.]

Your father opens the jar of honey. You notice a dead bee inside. The company placed it there as proof that the pure honey was collected from a honeycomb. In fact, the contents are neither pure nor honey. Dad is spreading his bread with glucose, a thick syrupy substance chemically produced from cornstarch. The bee is real.

The jam is tasty enough, although your mother assumed she was paying for something made from strawberries and sugar. Instead the jar is full of glucose, leftover apple pieces, a dangerous red dye, and salicylic acid to keep it from spoiling.

[Today, salicylic acid is an ingredient in wart remover, acne cleanser, and dandruff shampoo.]

Your little brother starts crying. He's cutting a new tooth. Mom gives him a spoonful of Mrs. Winslow's Soothing Syrup, guaranteed to calm a fussy baby. She has used it before, and it works. That's because the medicine contains morphine, a strong narcotic, which knocks out your brother for several hours.

Mrs. Winslow's Soothing Syrup was advertised as the best cure for diarrhea, colic, and all pain. This 1885 advertisement gave no hint that it contained the narcotic morphine.

For dessert, your mother places a yummy-looking cake on the table. To prepare it, she added baking eggs. Not only were they cheaper than the eggs she fries up for breakfast, but they were also older. Much older. She would have noticed the telltale odor of rotting eggs except that they'd been deodorized with formaldehyde.

Winking, Dad slips you a piece of candy under the table. Unknown to him, the candy company tinted it with arsenic- and lead-based colors.

[Arsenic and lead are not ideal treats for growing children. Arsenic causes digestive ailments. Lead affects the brain and nervous system.]

The tea steeping in your mother's cup isn't the expensive imported kind she expected. Leaves from various common trees and shrubs are mixed in. So are bits of wood, brick, and lead to increase the weight, costing her more for her fake tea.

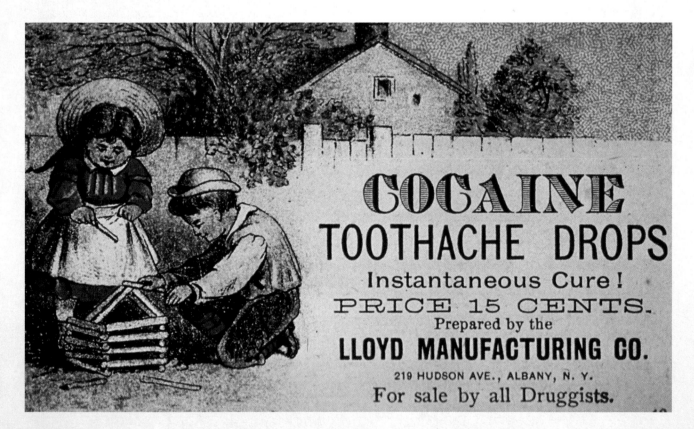

A popular toothache product for children was made with an addictive drug. The back of the 1885 advertising card pronounced: "this preparation of Toothache Drops contains cocaine, and its wonderful properties are fully demonstrated by the many recommendations it is daily receiving."

Your father thinks he's sipping coffee made from a special blend of coffee beans. The blend is really a combination of roasted and ground-up peas and acorns, with a pinch of charcoal.

Mom has no idea that she's serving the family these cheap substitutions and hazardous chemicals. The packages and bottles don't list the ingredients. She can only trust her nose and eyes to tell if the milk is sour, the eggs decayed, or the meat rotten. Food manufacturers have found ways to fool her.

⸻ ◆ ⸻

At the dawn of the twentieth century, few people had a clue that they were regularly being ripped off, drugged, and poisoned. A dedicated group of Americans recognized what was going on, and they set out to make food and medicines safer.

The battle would be long and frustrating. Victories were often unsatisfying. Before it was over, men, women, and children suffered and died. But eventually, the persistence and hard work changed our world.

The story begins where all our food once did—on a farm. This one was in Indiana.

CHAPTER TWO

FARM BOY

"I found myself more and more interested in chemistry and the science of nutrition."

—Harvey Wiley

Harvey Washington Wiley was the right person in the right place at the right time.

He was born on October 18, 1844, in a log cabin on a 125-acre southern Indiana farm. His parents struggled to feed and clothe seven children. Harvey was the sixth.

Almost everything the family needed came from their farm. For food, the Wileys grew corn, wheat, oats, barley, and rye, and they raised cows, chickens, and sheep. Horses pulled the farm equipment. The maple trees and sorghum cane crop provided sweet syrup. Lucinda Wiley spun and wove her family's clothing from the sheep's wool. The children were expected to help with farm chores.

Early in Wiley's childhood, the family moved from the log cabin where he was born to this farmhouse, which his father built nearby.

Harvey Wiley's parents: Lucinda Maxwell Wiley, born in Kentucky in June 1809 and died at age 83; Preston Wiley, born in Ohio in December 1810 and died at age 84.

THE SQUARE ON THE FLOOR

Harvey's father, Preston, earned extra money by plastering walls in new homes. He also was the church pastor and sometimes the schoolmaster.

The small farming community had no public school. Instead, parents paid a modest fee for children to attend a one-room schoolhouse. Classes only lasted three or four months during the winter, and students ranged from age six to teen. Four-year-old Harvey became an unofficial pupil when his father took him along so that he could keep an eye on the little boy. Preston Wiley drew a chalk square on the schoolhouse floor and told his son to stay inside the lines. Young Harvey obeyed. There was no other option in the Wiley household. He sat still, listened, and learned to read and do arithmetic with the older children.

Because the local school met only when enough parents paid the fee, Harvey spent just four winters in a schoolhouse before he turned eighteen. What he missed in mathematics, geography, writing, and spelling, he picked

Harvey (left), age nine, with his brother
James, age eighteen, in the summer
of 1854. James died two months later
from an accidental gunshot.

up on his own. He studied history and literature using books from his father's collection and the township library. Books opened the world to him. He even learned to play chess from one and taught his father and younger brother so that he'd have opponents. Chess became a lifelong passion.

KEEP OUT THE REBELS

The Wileys were abolitionists. Before the Civil War, Preston operated part of the Underground Railroad for slaves escaping from Kentucky across the Ohio River, five miles from the Wiley farm.

When war broke out in April 1861, Harvey wanted to volunteer in the Union army. His height and strong build made him look eighteen, but he was two years too young to enlist. He later said, "Because of my parental training in truthfulness I would not swear falsely as to my age."

Harvey and his father joined the local cavalry of the Indiana Legion, a group organized to defend the state from Confederate army attacks. The Wileys' company was charged with guarding the nearby Ohio River against Rebel troops coming from Kentucky.

For Harvey, the Legion didn't turn out to be as exciting as he'd hoped. Except for Saturday drill practice, their company only reported for duty if an alarm went up. Despite several enemy raids, Harvey didn't participate in any military action. The teen was always assigned to headquarters to carry messages.

By this time, Harvey knew he didn't want to be a farmer all his life. Although Lucinda and Preston Wiley had had little formal schooling, they valued education and encouraged their children to seek it. Even Harvey's three older sisters attended at least one year of college at a time when women rarely had that opportunity.

Hungry for more education than the rural community could provide, Harvey announced in spring 1863, "Father, I am going to Hanover College." The school was in a town five miles away.

His parents were supportive, as Harvey expected them to be. "Very well, son, go along!" Preston responded.

The decision brought challenges. Before eighteen-year-old Harvey could formally enroll, he had to pass the entrance exams. That meant taking extra instruction in Latin and Greek with a tutor at the college.

Since his family didn't have much money to spare, Harvey brought his food from the farm once a week and prepared it in his rented room in Hanover. He wore clothing his mother made. His father advanced him money for rent, and Harvey paid it back by walking home every Saturday to work on the farm.

Before regular college courses started in September 1863, he had passed the entrance tests and was ready. Harvey enjoyed his classes and new friends. He joined two campus literary societies (groups that held debates and presented speeches), gaining skill in public speaking that would later prove useful.

OFF TO WAR

As the Civil War continued that September, Harvey lamented the thousands of dead. But he felt confident that an end would come with the Union restored. He wrote in his diary, "Prepared 'to do or die' for cause so great."

Harvey Wiley, nearly nineteen, early in his freshman year at Hanover College, Indiana. According to Wiley's U.S. Army discharge papers in September 1864, he had black eyes and hair.

In early 1864, President Abraham Lincoln authorized short enlistments of one hundred days to attract more volunteer soldiers into the Union army as a way to increase troop strength and win the war sooner. Harvey saw his chance to serve during the summer before his second college year began in the fall. Along with many of his Hanover College classmates, he signed up in the Indiana Volunteer Infantry that May.

Harvey's infantry company was stationed in an area of Tennessee from which the Union army had pushed Confederate forces nearly a year before. The Indiana soldiers were responsible for guarding U.S. government supplies along the railroad.

Harvey was assigned to patrol duty. In his spare time, he studied human anatomy under his friend, a sergeant who had been a medical student before enlisting.

Although he witnessed no battles, Harvey saw plenty of illness. Writing in a pocket-sized leather-bound notebook, he kept a diary of his experiences. For a while that summer, his company was stationed close to a smallpox hospital. He wrote that they all were at risk of infection when the recovering patients, wearing "their polluted clothes," intermingled with the soldiers.

Halfway through his service, in July, Harvey broke out in red spots. He had measles, a highly contagious viral disease. Many enlistees, like Harvey, had grown up in isolated communities and had never been exposed to measles before joining the army.

Soon after he recovered, Harvey developed diarrhea, which was a frequent ailment in unsanitary camp conditions. He rejected what he considered the useless quack medicines that others took "with a faith that cannot be accounted for." Instead, he temporarily cured himself by fasting until his symptoms passed. But continuing bouts of diarrhea caused him to lose weight and become weak.

Looking back years later, Harvey realized that he probably had been infected with hookworm, an intestinal parasite spread through human waste. Then common in the southern states, a hookworm infection sapped its victim's strength and led to significant weight loss.

Corporal Harvey Wiley's hundred-day service ended in late September 1864. He finally could go home and resume his college studies. The Civil War would be over seven months later.

THE DOCTOR

By June 1867, Harvey had earned his undergraduate degree from Hanover College, graduating in a class of ten. He had been fascinated by his biology and chemistry classes, just as he had enjoyed his informal anatomy studies in the army. Medicine seemed like the right profession for him.

Now nearly twenty-three, he began an apprenticeship with his Civil War friend, who had since become a practicing doctor in Kentucky. Harvey read medical books and went along on patient visits, traveling the country roads on horseback.

Wiley in 1867, when he graduated from Hanover College, age twenty-two

After a yearlong apprenticeship, he signed up for formal medical classes at the Indiana Medical College in Indianapolis. As Harvey studied medicine, he saw that its practice was alarmingly unscientific, especially when it came to the drugs doctors gave their patients.

"This and that remedy were tried," he wrote later, "without much knowledge of pharmacology or the ulterior effects of drugs." These drugs interested him, and he took additional chemistry classes to find out more about them.

Harvey received his medical degree in spring 1871. The following year, the medical school offered him a position as head of the chemistry department. He would be taking over from the professor for whom he had been an assistant during his final year. Harvey turned it down. He knew his training wouldn't be sufficient for the job until he had studied more chemistry.

At science conferences he'd attended, Harvey had been impressed by several chemistry professors from Harvard University. He decided that Harvard was the best place for him to expand his knowledge. In September 1872, he headed east to Cambridge, Massachusetts, for another year of science classes.

His decision turned out to be a wise one, providing him the advanced courses he sought. As the academic year came to a close, Harvey sat for seventeen days of oral and written examinations to test his mastery of the entire four-year curriculum. He passed them all, and Harvard awarded him a Bachelor of Science degree. For the rest of his life, Harvey was proud of this achievement.

Armed with his Harvard degree, he returned to Indianapolis to teach chemistry and physiology at the Indiana Medical College. But one thing had changed. Practicing medicine, especially surgery, no longer had the appeal for him that it once had. "My aversion to shedding blood and causing pain was so great," he wrote, "that I felt I could never succeed in surgical practise."

THE SCIENTIST

In August 1874, Harvey was approached about a position as professor of chemistry at Purdue University, a new college right outside Lafayette, Indiana. His salary would be more than he had ever earned, and he jumped at the offer.

Having just opened, Purdue had enrolled only three dozen students for the fall semester. Thirty-year-old Harvey Wiley was the youngest of its six instructors. He was hired to train future farmers and engineers as well as to conduct research that supported Indiana's agriculture business. Harvey set up a new chemistry lab to investigate soil, water, plant crops, and fertilizers.

Always eager to enrich his knowledge, Harvey took a leave of absence from Purdue in 1878 to study in Europe. He visited hospitals and sat in on lectures in chemistry, physics, and pathology. What he learned changed the direction of his career.

In Germany, Harvey used equipment that analyzed the chemical composition of food. Scientists were beginning to examine how chemicals affected the health of humans and farm animals, and Harvey was intrigued. Although he didn't know it then, this research led to the discovery of vitamins more than thirty years later.

When Harvey returned to Purdue after several months away, he focused his laboratory studies on food products, particularly sugar. Food companies had been replacing naturally occurring sugar in their goods with an inexpensive substance made from cornstarch. As a chemist, Harvey knew how to combine cornstarch with water and acid to create the slightly sweet syrup called glucose.

These companies earned a tidy profit when they sold cheap glucose deceptively labeled as honey or maple syrup. Glucose was safe to eat. But its substitution cheated unsuspecting consumers and stole business from beekeepers and syrup producers. After investigating glucose in foods, Harvey reported the fraud to the Indiana State Board of Health and wrote scientific journal articles about it.

He uncovered other chemicals secretly being added to foods, too, some of them harmful. Harvey came "to believe that tremendous changes had to be brought about before there would be anything like the protection the public needed from impure and dangerous substances."

Harvey Wiley was determined to work for those changes, and he soon would get the chance.

CHAPTER THREE

CHEMICAL FEAST

"Poisonous adulterations . . . have, in many cases,
not only impaired the health of the consumer,
but frequently caused death."

—Alex. J. Wedderburn

nlike other instructors at Purdue University, Wiley was young, unmarried, and friendly with his students. He realized that he didn't fit the professor mold. One day in 1880, he found out that the university's administration felt the same way.

Wiley was summoned to a meeting of Purdue's board of trustees. When he arrived, one of them announced, "We have been greatly pleased with the excellence of his instruction."

Wiley hoped they were about to give him a raise as reward for his effective teaching.

The trustee went on, "We are deeply grieved, however, at his conduct." He explained that Wiley spent too much time with students outside of class—playing baseball. It was undignified.

"But the most grave offense of all has lately come to our attention," continued the trustee. "Professor Wiley has bought a bicycle . . . It is with the greatest pain that I feel it my duty to make these statements in his presence and before this board."

Well, that was going too far! Wiley's bicycle, with its large front wheel and small back one, proved to be his undoing.

"Gentlemen, I am extremely sorry that my conduct has met with your disapproval,"

Wiley told the group. "I desire to relieve you of all embarrassment on these points." He submitted his resignation on the spot.

The board of trustees refused to accept it. After all, Wiley was a highly capable professor. So he stayed, though he bristled under the administration's strictness.

THE DOC GOES TO DC

Wiley's sugar research caught the attention of other chemists, including those in Washington, DC. In 1883, he was offered a job in the U.S. Department of Agriculture's Division of Chemistry. Considering the awkward situation at Purdue, he didn't hesitate. In April, Harvey Washington Wiley took the oath as the Division's chief chemist.

The chemistry division developed and tested better farming methods, crops, and fertilizers. It also helped protect farmers from food deceptions, such as the substitution of glucose for natural sugars and syrups.

Wiley was part of rural, farming America. But he was part of the world of chemistry and medicine, too. He knew how science could be used to fool a customer.

Wiley posed for this portrait around the time he moved to Washington. He was a large man for his day, standing just over six feet and weighing more than two hundred pounds.

DEATH BY PICKLE

For centuries, unscrupulous people had been making money by tampering with food and beverages. They added cheaper materials or disguised rotten ingredients to appear fresh. These deceptions are called adulteration.

In 1820, chemist Fredrick Accum (1769–1838) published a book in London detailing the ways dishonest merchants adulterated food, beverages, and drugs.

Accum described how lead was added to cheap white wine to make it clear and seem like better quality. Even then, physicians knew that lead accumulated in the body over time and could cause death.

To look more appetizing, pickles were prepared by soaking the cucumber-vinegar mixture in copper pans. Copper leached into the pickles, turning them greener. Unfortunately, the amount of copper was enough to cause stomach pain, vomiting, or even death in a few pickle-eaters.

Bakers cheated customers by replacing wheat flour with inexpensive ground beans, peas, and chalk as a whitener. Some substituted sawdust for flour in bread.

By the second half of the nineteenth century, the business of adulteration had boomed. So had America.

After the Civil War, the United States changed dramatically. The railroad system expanded at a dizzying pace, connecting cities and towns and allowing people to travel to more places. Steamboats were speedier, making ocean travel easier and bringing more people to American shores. Cities swelled with European immigrants. Though the majority of Americans lived in rural areas, the urban population was rapidly increasing.

A cartoon appearing in *Puck* magazine in 1884 shows a chemist testing foods for adulteration. When Wiley took over the Division of Chemistry, concerns were rising about deceptive and dangerous foods.

Daily life for the average person had changed, too. During Wiley's youth, most families produced their own food. If they didn't have a certain item, they bought it from a neighbor. When someone sold poor-quality food, word spread in the small communities. People avoided buying from him again.

But by the 1870s, more and more Americans were living in towns and cities, where many worked at factory jobs. They no longer raised their own food or bought it from a friend. Instead, they shopped in stores stocked with cans of fruits, vegetables, and meats, not knowing where the food came from or who produced it.

CAN IT!

Delivering food to the public became a big business. Food manufacturers supplied stores across the country, shipping products hundreds of miles by railroad. Transporting food long distances took time. That meant the food had to be preserved so that it didn't spoil before customers received it. Cold temperatures prevent or slow down decay. Refrigeration was still being developed, however, and wasn't widely available for moving food.

Canning was the solution.

People liked using canned food. It needed less cooking and was quicker to prepare than fresh. A family could get even seasonal foods, like fruits and vegetables, in a can whenever they wanted and at reasonable prices.

There were problems, though. Unlike homegrown food, canned products were touched by many dirty hands between the farm and the processing factory. The foods often weren't fresh or clean when they were put into containers.

If bacteria are not destroyed during canning or bottling, usually by

Wiley (fourth from left) and several chemists and laboratory assistants take a break outside the Division of Chemistry's headquarters in 1885. The division's small staff worked on food and agriculture research in labs in the basement of the Department of Agriculture building.

heat, they have time to multiply before reaching the kitchen table. The food inside the container decomposes, and it can sicken the diner.

Decaying food smells and tastes foul, a warning that stops people from swallowing it . . . but only if they can detect it. Food manufacturers masked those odors and tastes by adding other substances. For example, sugar was used to hide the sour taste of spoiled corn.

During the late nineteenth century, new chemicals were developed that stopped the growth of microbes and slowed down decay. Many canners and food processors rushed to use these preservatives. No one knew what effect the chemicals might have on the human body, particularly in large quantities over a long period.

TURNIPS, PARAFFIN, AND CHARCOAL

When Wiley arrived at the Department of Agriculture in 1883, the Division of Chemistry had already been studying harmful and deceptive foods. He expanded the research. The chemists became detectives, exposing the true contents of foods and beverages.

Had the canner added a substance to preserve the food or to disguise decay? Had the food manufacturer substituted cheap filler, such as glucose? Under the microscope, cells look distinctive, making it easy to spot ground peas instead of coffee beans or to see mold contamination.

The Division published the results of its scientific tests, showing that nearly every type of food had been adulterated by at least one company. The report listed products that were ripping off or endangering consumers—often both at the same time. Wiley

In 1890, Wiley and his staff moved to this brick building across the street from the Department of Agriculture. The tracks embedded in the cobblestone are for streetcars.

estimated that about fifteen percent of food and beverages on the shelves had been tampered with.

Oleomargarine—made from vegetable oil, beef fat, lard, and yellow coloring—was being sold as genuine butter. Dairy farmers, who produced butter from milk, lost business.

Horseradishes sold in stores turned out to be less expensive turnips.

Sausages were made of ground decayed meat. The rotten food was disguised with coloring and spices.

To make rice look whiter and protect it from insects, manufacturers coated the kernels with glucose, talc, and paraffin. Talc is a mineral used in paint and powder. Candles are made from paraffin. The human body can't digest either one.

Candy contained ground marble to increase its weight. Customers who thought they were buying a pound of pure sweet confection were paying for stone bits, too.

Wiley and his team analyzed pepper samples that were composed

In 1893, workers at Armour's Chicago meatpacking plant use presses to extract oil from beef fat. The oil was turned into oleomargarine, a butter substitute. To deceive the customer, oleomargarine was sometimes colored yellow to look like butter.

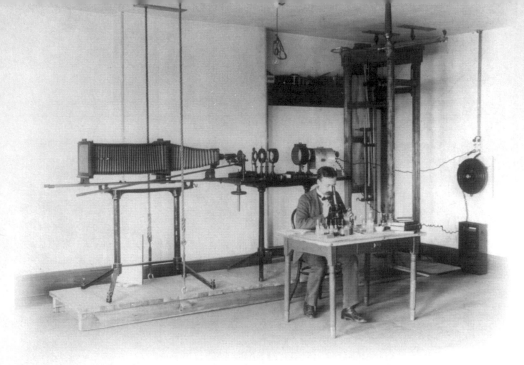

A scientist on Wiley's staff uses a microscope to analyze the makeup of a food sample. The equipment behind him produced highly magnified photographs.

mainly of ground corn, cracker crumbs, and charcoal . . . with scant amounts of real pepper.

Orange juice tested by one chemist was actually sweetened water with citric acid and extract of orange added for flavor. The manufacturer charged customers fifteen times what it cost to produce.

POISON COLORS

Substituting turnips for horseradishes cheated the buyer without injuring the body. But other adulterations involved substances that might cause physical damage.

Wiley was suspicious of chemical preservatives. Traditional preservatives such as salt, sugar, and spices were known to be harmless. They had obvious tastes so that a diner could tell when food had been preserved. But the new chemical additives had no taste or smell, especially in small amounts. A person was unaware of ingesting them. Wiley wasn't convinced they were safe.

Borax and boric acid sprinkled on meat and broken eggs stopped bacteria growth and covered up the smell of decay.

Saltpeter (potassium nitrate) was used to preserve meats. It held the red color so that the consumer thought the meat was fresher than it was.

Salicylic acid and sodium benzoate were added to bottled ketchup and canned tomatoes to stop overripe tomatoes from decomposing.

Wiley considered the common preservative formaldehyde a risky

Wiley's bicycle got him into trouble at Purdue University. In Washington, he bought a car and ran into trouble there, too. He and his steam-run 1900 Mobile were involved in one of the city's first car accidents. The distracted driver of a horse-drawn delivery wagon rammed into the side of Wiley's car. The horses and wagon were unscathed, and the driver sped away without stopping to see if Wiley was hurt. The car was badly damaged, but Wiley was only bruised.

chemical to eat or drink. Even worse, when formaldehyde was put in milk, it destroyed the bacteria that turned milk sour. Without the warning signs of foul smell and taste, a person couldn't detect the milk's age. But because formaldehyde didn't kill *all* the harmful bacteria in spoiled milk, the unsuspecting consumer became ill.

By adding preservatives, manufacturers got away with using rotting foods and unsanitary canning methods. Wiley argued that if companies used fresher ingredients and proper sterilization, they wouldn't need chemicals.

He distrusted food coloring, too. The first chemically produced food dyes were created in 1856. They were cheaper for manufacturers to use than natural plant dyes like paprika red. Because these new dyes were made from processed coal, they were called coal-tar colors. Wiley believed most were "highly poisonous and injurious" and dangerous for children.

Other food colors were made with mercury, a chemical that damages the brain and nervous system. The Division of Chemistry found arsenic in the red coloring used in meat and candy. One yellow dye contained lead and caused convulsions and death in dozens of people who ate cake colored with it.

"The practice of artificial coloring," said Wiley, "is reprehensible."

It bothered him that the poor suffered most from adulteration. They could only afford the cheapest food, which was usually the lowest quality, least nutritious, and most hazardous. "The poor man," he wrote, "while entitled to get a cheaper article, is likewise entitled, as well as the rich man, to protection against deleterious substances."

Something had to be done. His father had often told him: "Be sure you are right and then go ahead." Now Wiley was sure. The United States needed a law to keep its food pure and safe.

WOMEN RISE UP

Harvey Wiley wasn't alone in his concerns. A few European governments wouldn't allow certain American products to be sold in their countries. That hurt U.S. farmers.

To protect their farmers' business and their citizens' health, several state legislatures passed laws during the 1880s and 1890s to stop food fraud. But each state had its own rules. Even food manufacturers who used high-quality ingredients and no chemical preservatives had trouble complying with so many different state regulations. These companies preferred one federal law that applied to all states.

American women were keenly aware of the changes in food, too. While some—mainly unmarried women— had paying jobs, the majority worked within their home, managing the household, caring for family, and preparing meals. They knew that products on store shelves were inferior to foods grown and preserved at home.

Several groups of women spoke out about dangerous food. They were outraged that watered-down and contaminated milk was cheating children of nutrients and making them sick. Babies had died from bad milk. When government leaders failed to do enough about the situation, women mobilized.

The General Federation of Women's Clubs rallied their members to pressure the U.S. Congress for a national pure-food law. The women wrote letters to elected officials and influenced the male voters in their families.

The Woman's Christian Temperance Union backed a pure-food law that included controls on quack medicines. The WCTU believed people ingested high levels of alcohol, often unwittingly, because these products did not label it as an ingredient. Hostetter's Bitters, for one, was sold as an

The Woman's Christian Temperance Union warned against alcohol and other drugs in bitters, which were sold as health-boosters for children and adults. Brown's Iron Bitters contained cocaine.

herbal tonic to cure whatever ailed you, from stomachache to diarrhea. It contained as much alcohol as whiskey, gin, rum, or any hard liquor served at a saloon or bar.

Eventually, more than one million women joined the pure-food movement. They held meetings, invited speakers, and passed out pamphlets to publicize their cause. Professional women, including schoolteachers, doctors, and nurses, wrote articles for newspapers and presented public lectures. One of them was Dr. Elizabeth Wiley Corbett, Harvey Wiley's physician sister.

Besides women's groups, a pure-food law had the support of farmers, fruit growers, grocers, and companies that didn't adulterate their products. The demands for action grew louder.

CONGRESS CONSIDERS

A few politicians heard. These congressmen and senators introduced dozens of pure-food bills in the U.S. Congress, beginning in the 1880s. Wiley watched as, year after year, Congress let them die. Most were defeated in a committee and never made it to a debate and vote by the entire House of Representatives or Senate.

Harvey Wiley sits at his desk in the Division of Chemistry, June 1893. He signed Division documents as "Chief."

The Capitol, where the
U.S. Congress meets

HOW A BILL BECOMES LAW: THE BASICS

★ A member of Congress (either a representative or senator)
introduces the bill.

★ A committee of the congressional chamber where the bill was introduced
(House of Representatives or Senate) considers it. The committee holds
hearings, often asking experts to provide information and opinions.
The committee debates and votes on the bill.

★ Based on the committee's decision, the bill may move to the full House
or Senate for debate and vote.

★ If that chamber votes in favor of the bill, it is sent to the other chamber
for consideration.

★ Both chambers must approve the bill before it can be presented
to the president.

★ If the president approves and signs the bill, it becomes law.

*For more details of this complicated
process, see the U.S. Congress video
at **Congress.gov/legislative-process**.*

**The White House,
home of the president**

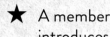

Meat-packers, canners, beverage companies, and some food manufacturers convinced members of Congress to oppose every bill. They claimed that their products were perfectly safe and that the quantities of additives were too small to cause health problems. In their view, a pure-food law amounted to unnecessary meddling in their businesses.

Wiley realized that compromises were needed to sway enough legislators to pass a bill. He hoped that a new law would, at least, slap punishments on cheaters. If a food or beverage contained preservatives, colorings, and flavors, he wanted the manufacturer to prove they were safe and to truthfully list the additives on a label. Then, he said, "the consumer will get what he wants, what he asks for, and what he pays for."

As the pure-food effort stalled in Congress, Wiley tried not to get discouraged. He felt more optimistic after William McKinley became president in 1897 and appointed James Wilson as agriculture secretary.

The new secretary encouraged research by Wiley and his chemists. Under Secretary Wilson, the Division of Chemistry's responsibilities expanded and more laboratories were set up. In 1901, it officially became the Bureau of Chemistry, and Wiley was its chief.

With the Department of Agriculture in support, Wiley used his position to push harder for the pure-food bill. He cultivated friendships on Capitol Hill. He gathered scientific evidence from his laboratory that congressmen and senators could use in persuading colleagues to vote for the bill. The lawmakers frequently called Wiley to testify before congressional committees as a science expert.

Wiley wasn't content to fight his battles in Washington. He traveled around the country giving public lectures to church groups, scientists, colleges, and farmers.

Despite his college debate experience and years as a teacher, Wiley had had a "terror of speaking in public" until he was thirty. But the more he faced audiences, the easier it became. As time went on, he learned to give a speech without the aid of a written version. "I never write out an after dinner speech," he told a Scranton, Pennsylvania, newspaper editor before one of his talks, "since I depend largely upon the local happenings of the dinner for what I have to say."

When Wiley gave a talk about pure food to a women's group, he often wore his top hat and tails. He dressed up to show them that their organizations were important. During such a speech in New Jersey, Wiley recruited one of his most effective and energetic allies.

Wiley and his staff on the steps of the Division of Chemistry building, around 1900. He often wore tails and a top hat to work when he was scheduled to give a luncheon speech to a women's group. Wiley was known as an entertaining and persuasive speaker.

THE "RUDE AWAKENING"

Alice Lakey first became interested in the pure-food movement in the late 1890s while caring for her father in Cranford, New Jersey. By 1903, she was in her midforties and a leader in its local organization. When Wiley

ALICE LAKEY (1857–1935) abandoned her dream of becoming a concert singer when she experienced poor health. She later taught voice lessons. As a leader in the pure-food movement, Lakey rallied other women. Although women could not vote in most states, they vigorously lobbied Congress to pass a safe food law.

spoke in Cranford in November of that year, Lakey introduced herself. Fired up by his speech, she joined the national fight.

Lakey was connected to several women's groups, including the New Jersey State Federation of Women's Clubs and its national organization. A member of the National Consumers' League, Lakey formed a committee to study food adulteration. She brought other women's associations to the movement, including the National Congress of Mothers.

To raise awareness, Lakey wrote articles for the newsletters of these organizations. She gave talks all over the country, sharing information that Wiley sent her.

In one speech, Lakey told a gathering in New York City about coffee containing clay and "the sweepings of the bake shops." She informed the shocked women, "Much of our grape jelly is made

A research chemist in a Bureau of Chemistry laboratory

of apple waste, glucose, and coal tar dye." She talked about a Boston baker who "used 1,000 pounds of bad eggs a day. These were deodorized with formaldehyde."

Lakey was confident that the pure-food movement would succeed. "A rude awakening," she wrote, "convinced [the average woman] that what she was feeding her family did not meet the standards of human decency."

Yet Wiley's speeches and the lobbying by women's groups and other organizations weren't enough. The opponents' voices were louder and more persuasive. Congress continued to vote down every pure-food bill that was introduced.

Wiley knew that without more support from the public, Congress would never pass a pure-food law. He believed that most Americans were still in the dark about the dangers in their food. There had to be some way to grab their attention.

Although Chief Wiley spent much of his time as an administrator, he enjoyed getting into the laboratory.

CHAPTER FOUR

The POISON EATERS

"We told them that they might receive some injury from it."
—Harvey Wiley

Wiley had been critical of food preservatives for nearly twenty years. He and other scientists suspected that the chemicals might disrupt normal digestion. Because a preservative slowed the breakdown of food *outside* the body, they reasoned, it could slow the breakdown *inside* the body, too. That would interfere with the release of food nutrients, compromising health.

Other food researchers said the opposite: the preservatives sped up digestion.

Wiley decided it was time to investigate exactly how the human body reacted to these chemicals.

SETTING UP THE EXPERIMENT

As a chemist, Wiley was accustomed to testing his hypotheses in the laboratory. "I arrive at my conclusions by experimentation, when experimentation can be used at all," he said. In 1902, he persuaded Congress to fund a study by the Bureau of Chemistry.

The questions he hoped to answer were: Do preservatives, colorings, and other food additives affect health? And if so, what quantities—if any—are safe?

He started with borax and its close relative boric acid. Food manufacturers added both preservatives to meats, butter, and milk to stop the growth of microbes. Dishonest companies also used them to disguise old foods as fresh ones.

Germany had banned American food containing borax based on an earlier experiment with two men. After eating various amounts of the chemical, the two suffered stomach irritation and diarrhea. Wiley believed that if his study found no danger, it would counteract the German research. But if borax proved harmful, it might convince manufacturers to stop using it and perhaps even rally the public and Congress behind a pure-food bill.

NONE BUT THE BRAVE

Wiley didn't think he could get worthwhile results from test animals because their digestive systems differed from humans. He needed human guinea pigs, preferably strong, healthy males. Wiley figured that a young man's body could better withstand the chemicals' possible ill effects. If those men were sickened by a preservative, then it "would naturally follow that children and older persons, more susceptible than they, would be greater sufferers."

He put out the call for young male volunteers within the Department of Agriculture. As part of the experiment, Wiley announced, they would be fed nourishing meals containing an addition of "ordinary preservatives and coloring matters used in foods." In return, all meals would be free, prepared and served in the basement of the Bureau of Chemistry building. For a young man living on a limited budget, that sounded like a good deal.

The volunteers were allowed to live in their homes and keep their regular jobs. Those who didn't work for the Department of Agriculture were paid five dollars a month so that they could be legally considered employees. A few applicants were medical students or had jobs in other government departments.

Of the men who put in their names, Wiley chose only those who were free of disease and illness during the previous year. He sought subjects who didn't use tobacco or alcohol regularly, but he couldn't find enough of them. He had to settle for including those who smoked, though they were required to record their tobacco use. He rejected anyone who consumed alcoholic drinks. Alcohol contains calories, which would complicate the experiment.

Twelve men made the cut. Most were in their twenties. Wiley later explained to a congressional committee, "We told them, of course, that there was no danger by poisons, but that there might be some disturbance to their systems."

Wiley and ten of the first dozen guinea pigs

The men had to commit to the experiment for at least six months and agree not to hold the government responsible if they became sick from the diet.

DIG IN

Once Wiley had his initial group of twelve subjects, he and his staff gathered preliminary information. One effect of the chemical additives might be weight loss. So they first determined the amount of food each man needed to maintain his normal weight.

For ten days at the beginning of the study, all the men were fed a healthy diet without preservatives. Each was weighed daily, and his food portions were adjusted to keep his weight steady.

The borax experiment began in December 1902. A cook prepared three meals a day. The menu rotated on a seven-day cycle and included a variety of meats, fruits, vegetables, and bread. A waiter served the volunteers at oak tables covered with white cloth. Wiley called them the Hygienic Tables.

All twelve men received the same foods. They had to eat everything they were served, "whether they wanted it or not." If a volunteer didn't eat his assigned portion, Wiley wouldn't be able to tell whether his weight change was due to the added chemical or to his food intake.

Wiley added a small amount of the chemical to butter, and then to milk and coffee. Although borax and boric acid are tasteless, the men soon realized where the preservative was hidden. They balked at eating that food, wrecking the experiment.

To guarantee that the volunteers ingested the measured amount of test chemical, Wiley put it in capsules, which the men swallowed with their meals. He thought the chemicals would mix with food in the stomach so that using capsules wouldn't affect the study.

At first, the dose of added preservative matched the amount typically found in butter and meat. Gradually, Wiley increased the quantity to find how much each man could tolerate.

COLLECT AND MEASURE

Bureau chemists assigned to the feeding study measured the weight and volume of everything the men ate or drank. They analyzed the food for water, fat, calories, and various chemicals.

For the human guinea pigs, though, the experiment wasn't quite as easy as simply eating. Each man had to fill out daily forms with his weight, pulse rate, and body temperature before and after meals. He recorded

Chemists analyzed the volunteers' food and waste. This photo was taken in a Bureau of Chemistry laboratory.

everything he consumed. He could eat only what he received at the Hygienic Table. If he was thirsty and drank water between meals, he had to measure and report the amount.

That wasn't the worst part. In order to find out if the test chemical interfered with digestion and if it passed out of the body, all the men's waste was measured and analyzed. The volunteers collected their urine in bottles and their feces in cans. Each day, they turned the excretions over to Wiley's lab staff.

A doctor from the U.S. Public Health Service examined the volunteers regularly, noting whether anyone showed symptoms from downing the preservatives. When someone felt too ill to continue, he was taken off the chemical and fed the same menu without it. Wiley's goal was to learn how much preservative created discomfort, not to overload or permanently damage the men's bodies.

Wiley assumed that any physical reaction was likely caused by the added chemical because that was the one thing that changed. If the ill man recovered after being off the test diet, Wiley considered it further proof that the preservative was the culprit.

The volunteers weren't sure how they would react to their new diet, and they adopted this slogan.

NONE BUT THE BRAVE CAN EAT THE FARE

Although he had many responsibilities as head of the Bureau, Wiley kept a close eye on the investigations. Early each morning, he walked two miles from his house to the basement kitchen. Arriving by seven, he often helped weigh the volunteers' portions. Then he sat down to eat breakfast with them. He ate lunch and dinner at the Hygienic Tables, too—without the borax or boric acid. When Wiley was away from Washington, his assistant W. D. Bigelow supervised the experiment.

Wiley (third from left) liked to eat with the volunteers. In front of him is a scale for weighing the served bread. The waiter (standing) brought food from the kitchen.

THE FAMOUS BOARDING HOUSE

When word of Wiley's investigation leaked out, a young *Washington Post* reporter, George Rothwell Brown, jumped on the story. Throughout the beginning months of the experiment, he visited the dining room regularly and wrote articles detailing the study's progress.

Brown even named some of the volunteers, called boarders in his articles. Though Wiley had kept their identities secret, Brown found out, probably by talking to the volunteers themselves.

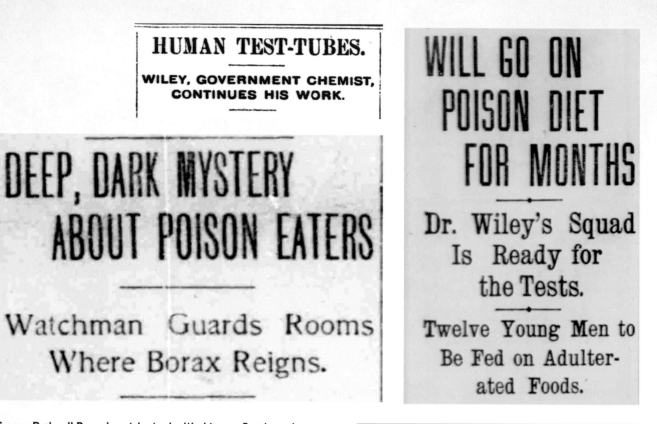

HUMAN TEST-TUBES.

WILEY, GOVERNMENT CHEMIST, CONTINUES HIS WORK.

DEEP, DARK MYSTERY ABOUT POISON EATERS

Watchman Guards Rooms Where Borax Reigns.

WILL GO ON POISON DIET FOR MONTHS

Dr. Wiley's Squad Is Ready for the Tests.

Twelve Young Men to Be Fed on Adulterated Foods.

WILL EAT ADULTERATED FOOD

Wiley's "Poison Squad" Reassembles on Monday Next.

George Rothwell Brown's articles in the *Washington Post* brought nationwide attention to the Poison Squad experiments. These headlines are from newspapers that picked up the story: the *Washington Standard* [Olympia, WA], March 31, 1905 (top left); the *Washington* [DC] *Times*, December 29, 1902 (bottom left); the *San Francisco Call*, October 12, 1903 (top right); and the *Bemidji* [MN] *Daily Pioneer*, January 7, 1905 (bottom right).

Headlines like "Second Day and No Fatality" and "Gloomy Christmas Dinner" grabbed newspaper readers' attention. Many of Brown's articles were total fiction, meant to be humorous. One mentioned that eating borax gave a pink tinge to the boarders' faces. Women wrote Wiley letters asking for more information about the new beauty aid.

Wiley was not pleased that Brown invented false details in order to tell an interesting story. He instructed his volunteers to stop talking to the reporter about the experiments.

But Brown continued to write his articles, and other newspapers picked them up. Soon, people across the country were reading about "poison eaters," "'poison' capsules," and the "poison squad."

Wiley didn't like the use of "poison." That made it sound as if he had already decided that the tested chemicals were harmful before conducting the experiment. Besides, the preservatives were not *poison*, a term that means *toxic*—causing serious harm or death, even in minute amounts.

He complained to the *Post* about the misleading articles and received a response from editor Scott Bone in late December 1902. "Our young man has not intended to be fanciful, but has aimed to make his stories readable, and in this he has succeeded." Bone referred Wiley's complaint to the city editor who, Bone promised, "no doubt . . . will respect your wishes."

Yet Wiley eventually saw the benefit of Brown's articles. News stories about the Poison Eaters reached millions of readers nationwide. Wiley had wanted the public to take notice of the chemicals in their food. Now they had. Dr. Wiley's Poison Squad became famous, and he started to use the nickname himself. He called his Hygienic Tables "the most widely advertised boarding house in the world."

Brown's articles put a human face on the issue of preservatives and pure food. Many people were interested in the volunteers who bravely agreed to test the chemicals, though others criticized Wiley for exposing the young men to risk.

> Philadelphia, Pa.
>
> Dear Sir:
>
> I read in the paper of your experiments on diet. I have a stomach can stand anything. I have a stomach that will surprise you. I am afflicted with 7 seven diseases. Never went to a doctor for 15 years. They told me 15 years ago that I could not live 8 months. What do you think of it? My stomach can hold anything,
>
> Yours truly,

Despite its nickname, the Poison Squad didn't scare off the volunteer who sent Wiley this letter. The man wasn't hired.

Newspapers called Wiley "Old Borax," and some made fun of his Poison Squad. One writer penned a song about it:

If ever you should visit the Smithsonian Institute,
Look out that Professor Wiley doesn't make you a recruit.
He's got a lot of fellows there that tell him how they feel,
They take a batch of poison every time they eat a meal.
For breakfast they get cyanide of liver, coffin shaped,
For dinner, undertaker's pie, all trimmed with crepe;
For supper, arsenic fritters, fried in appetizing shade,
And late at night they get a prussic acid lemonade.

They may get over it, but they'll never look the same.
That kind of a bill of fare would drive most men insane.
Next week he'll give them moth balls, a la Newburgh, or else plain.
They may get over it, but they'll never look the same.

THE VERDICT IS IN

The borax/boric acid experiment went on through five separate test periods until June 1903. In each period, the volunteers swallowed chemical capsules for about a month, then went back to eating the menu without preservatives.

Newspapers across the nation announced the beginning of Wiley's second series of experiments, on salicylic acid: the *New York Sun*, October 13, 1903 (top) and the *Evening Times-Republican* [Marshalltown, IA], September 17, 1903.

After those tests, Wiley and his staff continued the same experiments on different groups of volunteers using other food additives. For five years, until 1907, the Bureau of Chemistry tested sodium benzoate and the related benzoic acid, salicylic acid, sulfurous acid and sulfites, formaldehyde, copper sulfate, and saltpeter.

By the second year, more than two dozen Bureau employees—besides the preservative-eating volunteers—were assigned to work on the studies. That included eight chemists and their lab assistants, as well as five or six people who did the mathematical computing.

U. S. DEPARTMENT OF AGRICULTURE,
BUREAU OF CHEMISTRY.

DAILY CHART.

(To be filled out by each member of the Hygienic Table.)

Name and number: *Wm Pfunder # 2*

Date: *Wednesday Feb 8th 1905*

Temperature. (Sublingua.) F.°	Hour.	Pulse. (Beats per minute.)	Hour.	Weight, stripped. (Kilos.)	Hour.
98.4	540	73	540	65.61	525

| | STOOLS. | | Hour. | URINE. | Hour. |
Weight. (Grams.)		Consistence.¹		Volume, (c. c.)	

Symptoms: Normal, Pains, Colds, Feverish, etc.

Throbbing pains in the head dizzy - a little worse than yesterday

¹ Firm, soft, very soft, semiliquid.

Squad members filled out daily charts about their health. This volunteer's February 1905 report was from one of the unpublished investigations, either copper sulfate or saltpeter.

The volunteers reacted to high doses of the chemicals with stomach and intestinal pain, loss of appetite, headaches, and nausea. One young man recorded his physical symptoms on his daily chart: "Throbbing pains in the head; dizzy—a little worse than yesterday." The side effects lingered in some Squad members for several months until they regained normal appetite.

After the Bureau analyzed the experiments' results, Wiley concluded that the chemicals might not be dangerous in slight amounts. But he thought they could accumulate in the body, causing "disturbance to digestion and health." While a vigorous young person could tolerate high doses, Wiley feared that the sick and frail might not.

In what amounts could a preservative prevent food spoilage without harming diners? Wiley decided, "There can never be any agreement among experts or others respecting the magnitude of the small quantity." These chemicals shouldn't be used "where it can possibly be avoided." They never should be added, he argued, just because it was easier and cheaper for the food manufacturer. If a preservative did harm, it should be banned.

"I say, as a plain business proposition," Wiley reported to Congress early in 1906, "that the men who put preservatives in foods had better stop it for their good and for the good of their business."

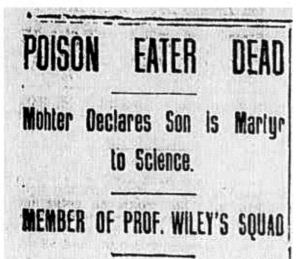

Robert Freeman's death was widely reported. This headline appeared in the *Daily Press* [Newport News, VA], November 23, 1906.

A CASUALTY?

In November 1906, twenty-three-year-old Robert Freeman died of tuberculosis in Washington. He had been in the first group of Poison Squad members from 1902 to 1903, and his shattered mother blamed her son's death on the experiment.

She claimed that Robert had been strong and healthy until joining the borax test. He developed tuberculosis soon after leaving the Squad, she said, likely because his body had been weakened by the "poisonous adulterants" in his food. She told a newspaper "that the Government or Dr. Wiley should pay damages for the death of her son."

When questioned by the press, Wiley denied that the Poison Squad had any connection to Freeman's illness. The young man had developed breathing trouble in January 1903, Wiley explained. When he didn't recover, he was dropped from the experiments that spring. At that time, tuberculosis was a leading cause of death in the United States, with its victims often younger than thirty.

Through January 1907, the Freeman story appeared on the front pages of Washington newspapers and some national ones, too. In one article, a newspaper reported on several congressmen who commented that "it is a bad practice to allow the lives of the citizens of the United States to be imperiled in any degree by any experiments with poisoned food."

Freeman's mother never filed a lawsuit, and nothing ever came of the accusation in Congress. His death apparently was a tragic coincidence. As far as history shows, none of the Poison Squad members suffered lasting effects from the experiment. At least one man lived to be ninety-four.

CRITICS SPEAK OUT

Wiley believed his tests showed that food preservatives could cause harm. But his experiments didn't impress everyone. Critics found many flaws.

One was the lack of a control group. If Wiley had stuck to his original plan, the twelve men would have been eating the same food at the same time in the same place. Six would have received the preservative with their food. The other six—the controls—would not. A volunteer wouldn't have known which group he was in. The physical complaints of the test group could have been compared to the controls. That would have indicated whether the chemicals caused the reactions.

But Wiley abandoned the initial procedure because it was less

The volunteers gather for a meal in the basement dining room at the Bureau of Chemistry.

convenient than feeding all twelve men the preservative at the same time. That eliminated the control group. Volunteers knew when they were being served the chemical additive. So did the people who served them; the doctors who examined them; the chemists who analyzed their waste; and Wiley, who ate with them. This might have influenced the experiment's results. Did the Squad members report dizziness or nausea because they *knew* they had ingested the chemical?

When Wiley started using capsules instead of mixing the chemical into food, he might have avoided this bias. He could have given out the capsules all the time to all the volunteers, even when they were getting chemical-free meals. The capsules could have been filled either with the preservative or with a harmless substance. The volunteers wouldn't have known which.

Another complaint about the experiments was that the analysis of the men's metabolism and body chemistry showed little change after they received a preservative. Did their nausea or stomach pain depend on the food they ate with the capsule, or the chemical itself?

In one test, Wiley reported that volunteers had headaches, sore throats, achy muscles, and losses of appetite. A critic pointed out that flu was common in Washington during that period and might have been the cause of these ailments. He charged that Wiley hadn't adequately controlled for outside illnesses.

UNCONVINCING

The Bureau's number crunchers computed experimental data with a Thacher Calculating Instrument. Patented in 1881, the device was used by scientists and engineers. The cylindrical slide rule was about eighteen inches long.

Skeptics also said the Poison Squad members weren't average consumers. Maybe women or children or older people would have responded to the chemicals differently.

A related objection was that Wiley used too few subjects. He responded that he would have preferred several dozen in each experiment, but he didn't have enough staff to handle the analysis of that much data. In his words, it was a "great mathematical labor of tabulating, computing, averaging, and studying the data for a period covering seven months."

Some detractors claimed that Wiley couldn't be certain his volunteers ate and drank only at the Hygienic Tables. Wiley argued that his chemists could detect an extra snack by analyzing the men's feces and urine. His critics weren't convinced.

Wiley expected criticisms from scientists working for the food preservative industry. But he received negative comments from fellow chemists, too.

When he gave a speech at the Chemists' Club in New York City in early April 1905, a Columbia University professor confronted him. The experiments didn't provide enough results to make conclusions, the man declared. Plus, they weren't ethical.

A Chicago chemist agreed: "Dr. Wiley is doing the best he can to frighten the public."

Another audience member warned that a pure-food law should not be based on Wiley's Poison Squad tests. "You could take any ten men," he said, "give

Scientific Martyrdom Of Poison Squad Over

Released From "Death Diet" in Various Stages of Wrecked Health---None Fatally Affected by Preservatives.

This headline appeared in the *Washington* [DC] *Times*, May 21, 1904, at the completion of the sodium benzoate study.

them something once a day for fifty days, and tell them that they were eating poison and at the end of that time they would all have lost flesh."

Wiley had never shied away from attacks. "I've been roasted before," he replied. "I'm perfectly willing to be here." Even though all food adulterations weren't harmful, he told the audience, it was morally wrong for manufacturers to slip them in. "If any American citizen wants a food product containing any preservative he ought to be allowed to have it, but I say that those who don't want such a product ought not to be deceived and compelled to take it."

Ordinary Americans didn't notice the flaws in Wiley's experiments . . . or care. They were disgusted and unnerved by the idea of chemicals in their food. The famous Poison Eaters had given the pure-food movement the boost it needed.

QUACK MEDICINES

Being fat was considered a sign of good health in the late 1800s. This 1895 ad (left) promoted fat as beautiful. The tablets and packaged food helped put on those attractive pounds.

But in the early twentieth century, being overweight was no longer stylish. The products changed to weight-loss nostrums. This one (right) promoted sanitized, jar-packed tapeworms to banish fat.

Harvey Wiley's research and speeches focused primarily on food dangers. But as a trained doctor and chemist, he had strong opinions about quack medicines, too. Newspapers, magazines, and even medical journals carried advertisements for nostrums to treat any ailment. Thousands of pills, syrups, and other remedies were available. Customers could buy them at a drugstore or through the mail, no prescription needed.

Sellers of quack medicines preyed on people with serious diseases, such as tuberculosis and cancer, which had no cures in the early 1900s. The drugs were cheaper than a doctor's visit, and the advertising made them sound effective and safe.

Children often fell ill with potentially fatal illnesses including measles, scarlet fever, and whooping cough. Anxious parents were willing to try any treatment that sounded promising. Fraudsters were glad to provide a tonic, pill, or elixir.

According to the 1889 advertisement, Dr. D. Jayne's Tonic Vermifuge cured everything from asthma to worms.

Most of the nostrums didn't cure or treat any disease. Many were addictive and downright harmful. The labels rarely stated what ingredients the user was swallowing.

"Poor mothers doped their babies into insensibility at night with soothing syrups containing opium or morphine," Wiley wrote. Some babies became addicted or died. He was frustrated that the public was not more concerned about "these glaring evils."

Before the Civil War broke out in 1861, sales of proprietary, or patent, medicines in the United States had been $3.5 million. By 1904, the business had exploded by twenty times to more than $70 million. With people buying so many quack medicines, Wiley set up a drug laboratory at the Bureau of Chemistry in 1903. The lab exposed the secret ingredients of numerous nostrums.

Physician and pharmacist organizations, as well as the Woman's Christian Temperance Union, urged Congress to add drugs to the proposed pure-food law. Wiley joined the call to require content labels on proprietary medicines. The consumer, he wrote, "should know the exact character of the product he buys."

In the 1880s and 1890s, colorful advertisements appeared on posters, in magazines, and on collectible trading cards. To catch the attention of concerned parents, the ads often featured children. This trading card for Dr. Seth Arnold's Cough Killer doesn't mention that the medicine contains morphine, a dangerous narcotic. Ayer's Pectoral (a medicine for respiratory ills) claimed to have been prepared by Dr. Ayer of Lowell, Massachusetts. Attaching a doctor's name to a quack drug convinced many buyers that it was safe and effective. Wistar's cough medicine, despite looking safe enough for children, contained alcohol and narcotics.

The superstition of modern Drug worship.

This 1901 *Puck* magazine cartoon pokes fun at Americans' belief that proprietary medicines will cure them of every ailment.

CHAPTER FIVE

MORPHINE, MEAT, and MUCKRAKERS

"The eyes of the people have been absolutely closed to the evils of this 'patent-medicine' curse."

—Edward Bok

The Poison Squad experiments had done more than make a few young men feel queasy and weak. By 1903, thanks to the publicity, people were aware of food adulteration in a way they hadn't been before. Even so, this awareness failed to result in a pure-food law.

Despite several bills being introduced in Congress, none passed. Lawmakers received political support and money for reelection from business groups that opposed the bills. Without significant pressure from the voters, most congressmen and senators saw no benefit to supporting the law.

The White House didn't push for any of the bills, either. In September 1901, President William McKinley had been shot dead by an assassin in Buffalo, New York. His vice president, Theodore Roosevelt, succeeded him.

Roosevelt had a reputation for advancing Progressive ideas to solve problems brought about by the country's shift from rural farming to urban industry. But he showed lukewarm interest in the pure-food bills.

Harvey Wiley had been unable to influence the new president to support the legislation. Late in his life, he wrote: "I fear that this man with whom I had many contacts after he became president never had a very good opinion of me."

SWEET DISAGREEMENT

The rift between the two men went back to the first months of Roosevelt's administration when the outspoken Wiley bumped heads with the strong-willed president.

Early in 1902, Roosevelt was trying to get legislation passed in Congress to lower the cost of importing sugar from Cuba. Wiley strongly opposed this idea. He had spent part of his career helping American farmers supply the nation's sugar. Cheap, foreign sugar would undermine these farmers.

During a hearing in the House of Representatives, a congressman asked for Wiley's views on the proposed bill. Wiley didn't hold his tongue. How could he lie to a congressional committee?

"I consider it a very unwise piece of legislation," he replied, "and one which will damage, to a very serious extent, our domestic sugar industry."

Wiley's answer made headlines. After President Roosevelt heard that a member of his own administration had publicly opposed him, he angrily ordered Secretary of Agriculture James Wilson to fire Wiley.

Wilson convinced Roosevelt that this was a mistake. Wiley had headed the Bureau of Chemistry for two decades. He was well-known and respected

PRESIDENT THEODORE ROOSEVELT (1858–1919) (opposite page) and Harvey Wiley were both strong-willed, opinionated men. At times, their personalities clashed. Roosevelt speaks to a crowd in 1903. Wiley's photograph was taken in 1910 at the Bureau of Chemistry.

throughout the country. Besides, Wiley hadn't expressed his opposition to the bill until asked directly.

Roosevelt cooled down, though he sent Wiley a message: "I will let you off this time, but don't do it again."

THE LADIES' MAGAZINE

As 1905 began, the campaign for a pure-food bill was at a dead end. Wiley had labored for twenty years to get Congress to pass a law. Yet he and his allies were no closer.

Two magazines changed everything.

Ladies' Home Journal was a popular magazine that printed stories, poems, and articles of interest to women. One million subscribers read it every month.

Editor Edward Bok became worried about reports of rising addiction to alcohol, morphine, opium, and cocaine found in proprietary medicines. Bok knew his audience: housewives who fed and nursed their families. Most had heard nothing about the harmful drugs in nostrums. Newspapers and magazines, which depended on proprietary medicine advertising money, rarely reported on it. The *Journal* refused those ads.

Bok hired young journalist Mark Sullivan to investigate the quack medicine business. In the May 1903 issue, the *Journal* advised readers against nostrums containing opium: "If the baby cries, and you are convinced he cries because he suffers, you must try to arrive at and remove the cause—not give him a 'soothing syrup' which may give both you and the baby a quiet half-hour at the cost of life itself."

A year later, the magazine published a list with the alcohol content of well-known tonics. The amounts were based on chemical analysis by the Massachusetts State Board of Health. Some of these quack remedies, widely used by women and their families, were nearly fifty percent alcohol.

In an accompanying editorial, Bok wrote: "Sooner or later the people of

In January 1898, the front cover of *Ladies' Home Journal* featured President William McKinley's wife, Ida, posing in the White House conservatory.

America must awaken to the fearful dangers that lie in these proprietary preparations. The mothers of our children, in particular, must have their eyes opened to the dangers that lurk in these patent medicines."

Bok acknowledged in the February 1906 issue that many women lived in rural areas and had no access to a doctor. When a mother's child was ill, she had no choice but to turn to a nostrum. "She has a right to know what she has paid for and what she is giving," he wrote. He urged passage of a federal food and drug law that forced companies to label the hazardous chemicals in their products.

NOSTRUM SECRETS

The editor at another popular magazine, *Collier's Weekly,* shared Bok's concerns. From the fall of 1905 through early 1906, Norman Hapgood published a series of exposés about the proprietary medicine industry. A few months later, the five articles appeared in a book called *The Great American Fraud.*

The articles' author was Samuel Hopkins Adams, a thirty-four-year-old investigative reporter known for his writings on public health and medicine. Adams collected nostrums and had them analyzed by a pharmaceutical laboratory and by his former chemistry professor at Hamilton College in New York. He interviewed state government chemists about the hazardous drugs they had examined.

Adams asked Harvey Wiley for help in his investigations. Wiley gave him information that the Bureau of Chemistry had collected in its testing, and he reviewed the drafts of Adams's articles.

The *Collier's* exposés turned the spotlight on more than 250 harmful or worthless proprietary medicines. Among them were Lydia Pinkham's

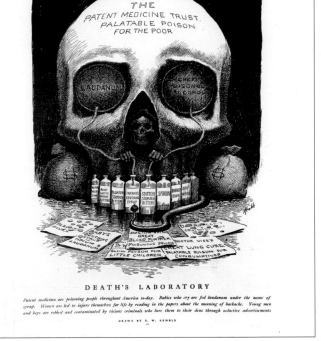

The illustration "Death's Laboratory," by E. W. Kemble, appeared in *Collier's* on June 3, 1905. The magazine uncovered the true nature of proprietary medicines.

One illustration in *The Great American Fraud* compared the alcohol content of a bottle of Hostetter's Stomach Bitters with that of several alcoholic beverages. The amount of alcohol in the bitters was nearly nine times that of the same volume of beer. The manufacturer's recommended dose of Hostetter's Bitters was two teaspoonfuls, several times a day. Some people drank much more than that.

ALCOHOL IN "MEDICINES" AND IN LIQUORS.

Vegetable Compound and Paine's Celery Compound. These liquids were marketed to women to "relieve[s] depression and lack of vitality." Many women who would never dream of drinking whiskey or beer were regularly downing these tonics, which had high alcohol levels.

"Even small doses of alcohol, taken regularly," Adams wrote, "cause that craving which is the first step in the making of a drunkard or drug fiend."

His articles stunned readers who had been unaware of the alcohol in the bottles on their bathroom shelves.

Adams criticized doctors who prescribed children's cough syrups and soothing tonics made with unsafe, addictive quantities of opium and cocaine. He reported cases of toddlers who died of heart failure after an overdose of cough syrup.

A mother he'd met gave her children Mrs. Winslow's Soothing Syrup, which contained morphine, so that she could go out with friends at night. One teaspoon and they "lay like the dead till mornin'," the woman said. Another mother of five children gave her youngest as much as an entire bottle of Winslow's in three days, addicting the baby.

Many of the quack medicines claimed to cure

Hydrozone, similar to Liquozone, claimed to kill germs safely. This advertisement, reproduced in Adams's *The Great American Fraud*, declares that Hydrozone will prevent and cure yellow fever. It could do neither. Today, the fight against the yellow fever virus involves a vaccine, mosquito control, and avoidance of mosquito bites. No drug has been found to kill the virus.

common illnesses (colds) as well as serious ones (tuberculosis). Liquozone, for example, promised to cure thirty-seven diseases, including tuberculosis, cancer, gallstones, influenza, and hay fever. Adams disclosed that the ineffective Liquozone was made of ninety-nine percent water with a splash of sulfuric acid. It was more likely to irritate a person's stomach than to cure him of thirty-seven diseases.

THE RED CLAUSE

The *Collier's* articles shamed magazines, newspapers, and medical journals for accepting advertising from the proprietary medicine companies. These ads used deceptive methods to attract buyers. Some said that the medicine was highly recommended by doctors. Others included testimonials from satisfied customers who had supposedly been cured by a particular nostrum. These endorsements looked like genuine news articles. Most were fake, written by the quack medicine company.

According to Adams, the nostrum firms were also guilty of manipulating news reporting. When a company offered to advertise in a newspaper or magazine, it inserted the red clause into the contract. The term came from the ink color sometimes used by the

An illustration from *The Great American Fraud* shows a window exhibit from a Chicago drugstore. Adams's investigation found that druggists didn't always resist the proprietary medicine companies, despite knowing that many of the concoctions were worthless. The majority of the average drugstore's business was nostrum sales.

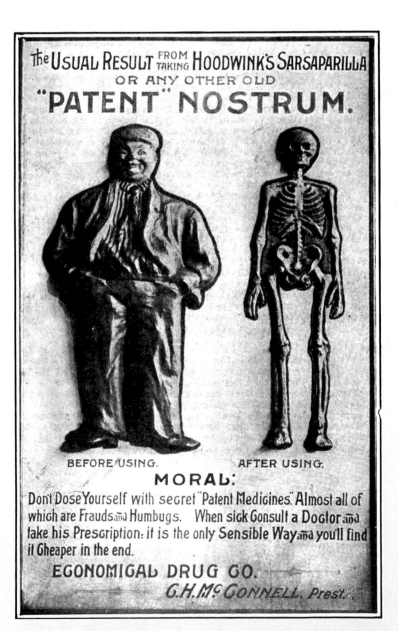

advertiser to write it in. The clause stated that the company would cancel its advertising contract if any laws—state or national—were passed that restricted the proprietary medicine business.

The blackmail worked. The news media depended on this income. Many gave in, printing articles and editorials that opposed food and drug laws.

If a newspaper refused to cooperate, its name was shared with other proprietary medicine companies. The newspaper's advertising revenue, worth thousands of dollars, dried up.

SHOCKING!

Readers of *Ladies' Home Journal* and *Collier's* were alarmed by the exposés. Women's groups, including the Woman's Christian Temperance Union and General Federation of Women's Clubs, flooded congressional offices with letters, telegrams, and petitions. Alice Lakey, several state food commissioners, and representatives of the American Medical Association together met with President Theodore Roosevelt to push for a food and drugs bill.

Roosevelt had stayed quiet about pure-food legislation. But the public mood was shifting. Above all, Roosevelt was a shrewd politician. In his annual message to Congress in December 1905, he recommended "a law to regulate interstate commerce in adulterated or misbranded food, drink, and drugs."

After Roosevelt's statement, a bill finally started to move through Congress.

Many women are denied the happiness of children through derangement of the generative organs. Mrs. Beyer advises women to use Lydia E. Pinkham's Vegetable Compound.

Lydia E. Pinkham's Vegetable Compound was advertised in newspapers nationwide. This ad is from the October 7, 1904, issue of the *Starkville* [MS] *News*. According to women's testimonials in these ads, the medicine cured female complaints, including miscarriage, kidney problems, tumors, and backache. The promises were fraudulent. Unknown to customers, the tonic contained twenty percent alcohol, which intoxicated many women.

Harvey Wiley kept up the pressure, rallying support for the bill even from unlikely allies. In mid-February 1906, he was invited to speak to a convention of canned goods manufacturers in Atlantic City, New Jersey. Many canners were against a national law, fearing that strict rules would increase their costs and crush their businesses.

Traveling from Washington by train, Wiley was met at the station by the group's president. The man blurted out, "I am frightened for your safety." The group is hostile to you, he told Wiley. You should turn around and go home on the next train.

Wiley was not one to run from a challenge. "I have never been mobbed," he replied, unfazed, "and perhaps it would be an experience worth having."

Later that day, when Wiley was introduced to the audience, no one clapped. He stepped forward to speak. The crowd was dead silent.

Staring out into the unfriendly audience, Wiley began talking without notes. "Is there a man in this audience who would put his hand in his neighbor's pocket, take a dollar from it and put it in his own pocket? If there is such a person let him hold up his hand."

No one reacted.

Wiley continued, "Is there a man in this audience who would so adulterate, so degrade and so misbrand a package of his goods as to cheat the consumer out of a dollar of his money when he bought that package? If so, hold up your hand."

Nobody raised a hand. Then someone clapped, and soon the entire audience joined in.

Wiley had their attention now. He went on to explain how a pure-food law would prevent those kinds of unethical practices. The law, he argued, would benefit his audience by stopping the cheats who undercut the honest businessman's prices.

He spoke for an hour, and at the end, received enthusiastic applause. The canners' organization soon threw its support behind the pure-food legislation.

THE SENATE VOTES

As the Senate debated the bill in early 1906, Wiley's name came up. He had become the face of the pure-food movement. His enemies didn't want the Bureau of Chemistry enforcing the new law. They expected Wiley to be tough on them.

The owner of a company that produced pickles and ketchup testified before a Senate committee. It would be a mistake, he said, to "give one man the absolute power to say what the manufacturers of this country shall do and what they shall not do."

A Rhode Island senator objected to Wiley's influence, too. "Are we going to take up the question as to what a man shall eat and what a man shall drink, and put him under severe penalties if he is eating or drinking something different from what the chemists of the Agricultural Department think desirable?"

A North Dakota senator responded with support for the bill. "It is the purpose of the bill that he [a man] may go into the markets and when he pays for what he asks for that he shall get it, and not get some poisonous substance."

In the end, the Senate passed the Food and Drugs bill on February 21, 1906, with sixty-three votes. The Rhode Island senator was one of twenty-two who abstained from voting. The four nays were from southern Democrats unhappy about increasing the federal government's power over the states.

But the pure-food bill stopped dead in the House of Representatives. There wasn't even a vote.

Then came the dirty meat.

THE JUNGLE

American author Upton Sinclair wrote novels and articles that promoted socialism. Having earned little money from his writing, he convinced a socialist weekly newspaper, *Appeal to Reason,* to pay him an advance to write a novel. The newspaper would publish the novel in sections.

Sinclair planned a story that showed how meatpacking companies took advantage of poorly paid workers, many of whom were recent immigrants.

In the fall of 1904, twenty-six-year-old Sinclair
traveled to Chicago to do research. He spent
seven weeks living among these workers and
recording the stories they told him.

Posing as a worker, Sinclair sneaked into
the stockyards and meatpacking plants. He
watched how hogs and cows were turned into
sausages, lard, bacon, and canned beef,
collecting vivid details for his novel.

Shortly after his fiction appeared in
Appeal to Reason, Sinclair made a deal to
have the novel published in book form. It was
released in February 1906, dedicated "To the

Workingmen of America." *The Jungle* was a worldwide bestseller and was translated into seventeen languages. Sinclair became famous.

It wasn't his socialist theme that grabbed readers, however. Instead, they were shocked at his graphic descriptions of meatpacking plants.

Rumors of abuses in the industry had circulated for several years. The word was that companies were using diseased animals in their canned meat. Government inspectors had not noticed this, or at least they had not reported it. *The Jungle* seemed to confirm these appalling reports.

Sinclair added the graphic passages to his book for realism, not expecting the reaction he received. The details only took up about a dozen pages of more than three hundred in the novel. But they were so striking that they jumped out at readers.

The factory "floor was half an inch deep with blood." Meat, poisoned rats, and rodent feces were mixed together and ground into sausage. Scraps of meat were shoveled off the filthy floor "where the workers had tramped and spit uncounted billions of consumption [tuberculosis] germs," then combined with the rest.

One of the most gruesome sections told of men who "fell into the vats; and when they were fished out, there was never enough of them left to be worth exhibiting,— sometimes they would be overlooked for days, till all but the bones of them had gone out to the world as Durham's Pure Leaf Lard!"

Sinclair's packinghouse story made headlines. The *New York Evening Post* printed a rhyme:

Headline from the March 10, 1906, edition of the weekly newspaper the *Chicago Eagle*. The article repeated horrifying details from *The Jungle*, including how meat from animals sick with tuberculosis and cancer was sold to American consumers.

Mary had a little lamb,
And when she saw it sicken,
She shipped it off to Packingtown,
And now it's labelled chicken.

The nation was horrified . . . and nauseated. Meat sales plummeted. Sinclair later wrote: "I aimed at the public's heart, and by accident I hit it in the stomach."

MOMENTUM

To many, the meatpacking scandal was more proof that America needed a law to protect its people from fraud and harm. After receiving hundreds of outraged letters from the public, President Theodore Roosevelt ordered an investigation into the stockyard conditions. He demanded to know whether or not the novel's details were accurate.

For the most part, they were. Even though a label said the meat had been inspected and passed by the U.S. government, the inspection was minimal.

Roosevelt knew something had to be done about the scandal immediately. Otherwise, European nations wouldn't trust U.S. government inspection and might refuse to buy American meat. The president wasn't on the sidelines anymore. He used his influence to push Congress into strengthening meat inspection.

The Jungle's revelations injected energy into the struggle for the Food

THE REAL PACKINGTOWN —
IF YOU LET THE PACKERS TELL IT.

The meat-packers argued that Sinclair's stories about their business were exaggerations. In July 1906, *Puck* magazine mocked the meat-packers' claim that they took excellent care of livestock before slaughtering them.

and Drugs bill, too. Supporters intensified their pressure on the House of Representatives, where the bill was stuck. In mid-June 1906, Alice Lakey wrote an impassioned letter to the editor of the *New York Times* on behalf of the National Consumers' League. Lakey admonished the House for ignoring the 750,000 women who had worked for the law. "Is this no longer a Government by the people, for the people, and of the people," she wrote, "but by the corporations for the corporations?"

The public outcry knocked down opposition to the bill in the House. During debate, a congressman from Buffalo announced to colleagues, "The people are demanding pure food."

On June 23, the House joined the Senate in passing the Food and Drugs bill. Congress also passed the Meat Inspection Amendment, giving the federal government new powers to inspect meat, control sanitation in packinghouses, and destroy unsafe products.

A week later, on June 30, 1906, President Roosevelt signed both into law. Newspaper headlines heralded the moment: "A Pure Food Law at Last" and "Pure-Food Bill Wins."

VICTORY . . . FINALLY

Harvey Wiley and his allies had fought for this legislation for nearly a quarter century. More than one hundred bills had been introduced in Congress and failed.

It had taken the coordinated action of numerous groups to get the law passed. Wiley gave credit to state food commissioners and chemists, national associations of doctors and pharmacists, and public health officials. He applauded the muckraker journalists Edward Bok, Mark Sullivan, Norman Hapgood, Samuel Hopkins Adams, and Upton Sinclair. Their writing exposed the truth behind proprietary medicines and unsanitary food manufacturing.

Above all, Wiley acknowledged the contribution by the hundreds of women's clubs and groups across the country who were, he later wrote, "the greatest and most forceful" organizations that advocated for the Food and Drugs Act.

Although Harvey Wiley was just one of many people who promoted its passage, he was recognized as the movement's point man. One Washington newspaper called him the "Relentless Foe of All Who Deal in Adulterations."

From his position within government, Wiley had been able to propel the effort. At his direction, the Bureau of Chemistry tested, uncovered, and publicized dangers and deceptions in food and drugs. He provided scientific information to congressmen and senators attempting to get bills through Congress. Through his engaging speeches, Wiley raised public awareness. He recruited and encouraged others to persuade lawmakers.

For all of that, he became known as the Father of the Pure Food and Drugs Act, later called the Wiley Act in his honor.

Wiley wrote in his autobiography: "How does a general feel who wins a great battle and brings a final end to hostilities? I presume I felt that way on the last day of June, 1906."

MUCKRAKERS

Illustration from the February 21, 1906, issue of *Puck* magazine, called "The Crusaders." Muckrakers are portrayed as knights battling social problems and corruption. Among those included are *Collier's Weekly* magazine, its editor Norman Hapgood, and writer Samuel Hopkins Adams.

EDWARD BOK
(1863–1930)

MARK SULLIVAN
(1874–1952)

NORMAN HAPGOOD
(1868–1937)

SAMUEL HOPKINS ADAMS
(1871–1958)

UPTON SINCLAIR
(1878–1968)

This page and opposite page: Two cartoons honor Wiley after Congress passed the Food and Drugs Act. He liked these enough to keep them with his private papers.

CHAPTER SIX

"JANITOR of the PEOPLE'S INSIDES"

"No honest man need lose a night's sleep over this new law, but dishonest men are losing several right along."

—Harvey Wiley

The promoters of pure food and drugs didn't get everything they wanted in the new law. But in Wiley's opinion, it was better than no law at all.

The Act made it illegal for manufacturers of food and beverages to put misleading claims on a label. They couldn't list ingredients that weren't there, water down a product, or mix in cheap substitutes. Companies weren't allowed to add poisonous and unsafe substances or disguise

SIR DEATH—YE KNIGHT OF IMPURE FOOD,
BY NOBLE KNIGHT SO HOT PURSUED,
NO LONGER WEARS IN MERRIE MOOD
"YE SMILE THAT WONT COME OFF"

IMPURE FOOD

CHEMICAL ANALYSIS

WILEY'S PURE FOOD

decomposing ingredients. Harmful colors and minerals were banned from candies.

The federal government now had the authority to test foods, including those shipped in and out of the United States. Officials could inspect manufacturing plants. If a company broke the law, it could be fined and its products seized.

BUYERS REACT

After reading about the Poison Squads and the new law, the public had become wary of preservatives. Consumers didn't want food products made with borax, formaldehyde, salicylic acid, and copper sulfate. They saw these added chemicals as signs of inferior or contaminated ingredients.

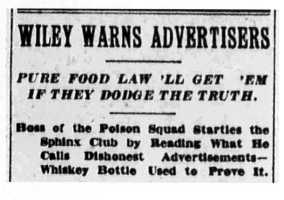

Wiley continued to give speeches about violations of the 1906 Act. This headline is from the *New York Sun*, November 11, 1908.

In response, food manufacturers adjusted the way they prepared their products. Even those companies that had opposed the pure-food bills went along with the changes. They began using better sanitation and sterilization methods that didn't require as many chemical additives.

The law also took aim at the dangerous chemicals in proprietary medicines. If a nostrum contained any of eleven specific drugs that could cause addiction and death, its label had to say so and state the drug's percentage of the product. The list included alcohol, morphine, opium, heroin, cocaine, and six additional drugs.

Mrs. Winslow's Soothing Syrup was forced to label its morphine. Hostetter's Bitters had to tell the amount of alcohol in the bottle.

The Act didn't end the sale of these medicines. It only controlled their labeling. Many consumers, now aware of what was in the nostrums, stopped buying them. In the wake of the law's passage, some companies changed their products. Mrs. Winslow's Soothing Syrup cut down on the morphine and, eventually, eliminated it.

Other than those eleven drugs, however, proprietary medicine companies didn't have to list ingredients. Plenty of quack remedies with hazardous contents remained on the market.

THE INSPECTORS

On January 1, 1907, the Act went into effect. Despite protests from Wiley's enemies, it put the Bureau of Chemistry in charge of examining foods and drugs and determining whether a company had broken the law. Wiley needed inspectors to track down illegal products.

By spring, he had hired twenty-eight inspectors from more than a thousand who applied. They had a range of backgrounds in law, medicine, pharmacy, and chemistry. After interviewing the men, Wiley chose twenty-nine-year-old Walter Campbell, a Kentucky lawyer, as chief inspector.

During their training, the inspectors visited factories to see how foods were processed. They learned to spot unsanitary conditions and to gather samples of foods and medicines from stores and factories. Because the

Bureau of Chemistry inspectors gather in Buffalo, New York, in July 1909. The number of inspectors increased from twenty-eight in 1907 to forty-four in 1913.

law didn't require the owner to let them examine company records, the inspectors had to be stealthy and observant.

Did a product's label deceive the consumer? Did the food include the ingredients it claimed on the package? Were any ingredients harmful? If it was a drug, did it contain one of the eleven dangerous chemicals, and were they listed on the box or bottle? Was the strength properly labeled?

Wiley told his inspectors to follow the motto: "When in doubt protect the consumer."

That summer, the twenty-eight men left for their posts in different regions of the country. After collecting samples for analysis, inspectors sent them to one of six Bureau laboratories set up in Boston, New York, Philadelphia, New Orleans, Chicago, and San Francisco. Within the next two years, fifteen more laboratories opened in other cities.

When the Bureau found a violation of the law, it was reported to the Secretary of Agriculture. Secretary Wilson had the power to turn the evidence over to the U.S. Justice Department for prosecution in court before a judge. The company's owner could be fined or jailed.

From the beginning, Wiley recognized the law's shortcomings. It had been weakened by compromises necessary to gain enough votes to pass Congress. He assumed that he and the Bureau of Chemistry could overcome those issues. Wiley expected that the inspectors' and chemists' findings would dictate which products were allowed and which were not. And once they did, the manufacturers would willingly comply.

He was wrong.

OUT-VOTED

In April 1907, Secretary Wilson set up a three-person Board of Food and Drug Inspection, ignoring Wiley's objections to it. This board made decisions about violations and recommended to Wilson how to apply the law.

Wiley was the head of the committee, but he was regularly out-voted by the other two members. Time and time again, after the Bureau of Chemistry identified an adulterated product and suggested legal action, the Board overruled that advice.

A photographer followed one of the original inspectors as he checked factories in the Baltimore-Washington area, around 1910–12. John Earnshaw, in dark suit and tie, visits a creamery. He looks for milk that has been watered down, adulterated with chemicals, or contaminated with bacteria.

Inspector Earnshaw stops at an egg processer. He examines the building's sanitation, the condition of the eggs, the employees' health, and the possible illegal use of chemicals to color or preserve the eggs.

In 1909, an inspector spotted moldy and wormy raisins in Washington, DC, bakeries. A court condemned them under the 1906 Act. In this photograph, the raisins are being destroyed.

John Earnshaw inspects a candy factory where Easter eggs are being prepared. Unlike some food-processing factories, this one is clean.

Earnshaw checks conditions at a Baltimore spinach processor.

Secretary Wilson wouldn't permit publication of Wiley's Poison Squad studies on copper sulfate and saltpeter. Based on those experiments, Wiley had concluded that the two chemicals were harmful to health and should be banned from food. But Wilson made sure that the results remained hidden from the public.

Wiley believed that the secretary and the two Board members were protecting companies that broke the law. Since 1897, he had gotten along well with Wilson. Wiley respected the man's ability and political skills. Yet he was disappointed in the secretary now. "He had the greatest capacity of any person I ever knew," Wiley wrote in his autobiography, "to take the wrong side of public questions, especially those relating to health through diet."

Wiley in a Bureau of Chemistry laboratory in 1907

THE IDIOT

Wiley made things worse for himself and the Bureau of Chemistry by once again locking horns with President Theodore Roosevelt.

In early 1908, Roosevelt called Secretary Wilson and Wiley to the White House to meet with a delegation of food manufacturers. The companies wanted permission to use sodium benzoate and saccharin in canned vegetables. They were there to convince the president of their position.

Wilson and Wiley were led into the room used for cabinet meetings. The delegation was already seated around the table. The president turned to Wiley. "Do you think the use of benzoate of soda in foods is injurious?" he asked.

"I do not think; I know," Wiley declared. "I have tried it on healthy young men and it has made them ill."

Dramatically, Roosevelt pounded the table and announced to the businessmen, "Gentlemen, if this drug is injurious you shall not put it in foods."

What about saccharin? asked one of the men, who ran a company that canned corn. "My firm saved $4,000 last year by using saccharin instead of sugar."

Wiley could not restrain himself. He had long suspected that saccharin, a substance derived from coal tar, was harmful. "Yes, Mr. President," he burst out, "and every one who eats these products is deceived, believing he is eating sugar, and moreover the health is threatened by this drug."

Roosevelt glared at Wiley. "Anybody who says saccharin is injurious is an idiot. Dr. Rixey [the president's physician] gives it to me every day."

Wiley saw that his comment had been a major blunder. He guessed that Rixey prescribed saccharin to lower Roosevelt's sugar intake and risk of diabetes. Now he was in hot water.

END OF THE POISON SQUADS

Two days later, the president ordered the formation of a committee of five university scientists to review Wiley's recommendations about violations. The head of the group was chemist Ira Remsen, president of Johns Hopkins University in Baltimore . . . and one of the discoverers of saccharin.

Unless the Remsen Board recommended prosecuting a company, the findings of the Bureau of Chemistry's inspectors and chemists were ignored. Secretary Wilson told Wiley to stop the Bureau's investigations of food additives. The Remsen Board would do future testing.

Wiley had always had opponents in Congress, and they were glad to cut off funding for his Poison Squad studies. The *New York Sun* applauded the cuts, too. Its editors questioned the cost to the taxpayers of "tests and investigations of every conceivable thing under the sun." They went on to doubt that "tests when made by a Federal Department are as authoritative as those of the university or scientist's private laboratory."

Later, Wiley remarked that his comment about saccharin to Roosevelt "was the basis for the complete paralysis of the Food Law."

Wiley may have been correct in thinking that his relationship with the president had hindered the law's enforcement. Although Roosevelt gave credit to Wiley for securing the Act and believed him to be a man of integrity, he distrusted Wiley's opinion.

Chemists and assistants at the Bureau of Chemistry, around 1910

In January 1909, the president wrote, "The trouble with Dr. Wiley is, that to my personal knowledge, he has been guilty of such grave errors of judgment in matters of such great importance as to make it quite impossible to accept his say-so in a matter without a very uneasy feeling that I may be doing far-reaching harm to worse than no purpose."

DASHED HOPES

Wiley anticipated better days when William Howard Taft was elected president in 1908, replacing Roosevelt. Taft gave every indication that he supported the Food and Drugs Law. He wrote in a letter: "I expect to give Dr. Wiley the reasonable and just support that he is entitled to have. But when I feel that he has done an injustice I expect to differ with him even at the expense of having my motives questioned."

As time went on, Wiley decided that Taft was no better than Roosevelt in resisting the enemies of the 1906 Act.

During the first three years of the law, the Bureau inspectors sampled thousands of products. According to Wiley's count, his chemists found hundreds of examples of fraud and adulteration. But the Board of Food and Drug Inspection and the Remsen Board disagreed. They recommended few of the cases to Secretary of Agriculture Wilson for prosecution. Wiley was critical of the Remsen Board's scientific tests, including those that claimed preservatives such as sodium benzoate were safe.

Wiley felt he had lost the war. In his view, dishonest manufacturers had gotten their way, and harmful foods and drugs were still allowed. His influence as chief of the Bureau of Chemistry had been eroded. "It was not a difficult law to understand," he wrote, "but it was an easy one to overthrow."

Through it all, Alice Lakey remained supportive. She wrote to Wiley reporting on her lobbying efforts against companies trying to get around the 1906 law. Lakey called the proprietary medicine makers "a cowardly lot of rascals."

She sympathized with him for his struggles with his enemies within the Department of Agriculture. "YOU ARE RIGHT. THE FUTURE WILL PROVE IT," she wrote. "You are the ONE MAN in Washington who has stood for the RIGHTS OF THE CONSUMER FROM THE BEGINNING."

PRESIDENT WILLIAM HOWARD TAFT (1857–1930) was elected in 1908, the year this photograph was taken. He later served as chief justice of the Supreme Court from 1921 to 1930.

THE REFRESHING "LIQUID BREEZE"

In 1911, Wiley was encouraged that at last he'd see one major adulterator brought to justice—Coca-Cola. For years, he had been concerned about beverages containing cocaine and caffeine, both addictive substances. Before the funding for the Poison Squad investigations was cut, Wiley planned to run human experiments on soft drinks.

Coca-Cola had removed cocaine from its special formula by 1903.

In this early 1900s advertisement, customers enjoy Coca-Cola at a soda fountain. The beverage started out as a medicinal tonic containing cocaine to treat fatigue and stimulate the brain. By 1903, it was marketed as a soft drink for people of all ages . . . without the cocaine.

Although Wiley knew that, he continued to call the beverage habit-forming because of its caffeine. He wanted to take action because Coca-Cola was the country's most popular soft drink and many children drank it.

Wiley unrelentingly pushed the case to Secretary Wilson. Finally, Wilson gave in. The U.S. government charged Coca-Cola with adulteration for adding a harmful ingredient (caffeine) to the drink. The company was also accused of misbranding because the name led consumers to believe the beverage contained coca and cola. It actually had no cocaine (from coca plant leaves) and scant amounts of cola (from the kola nut).

The case went to court in Chattanooga, Tennessee, where the company had its main bottling operation. The three-week trial in March 1911 featured testimony from doctors and scientists who studied caffeine. Wiley didn't testify because he hadn't done any experiments. But he attended the trial, taking along his new wife, Anna.

The government's expert witnesses testified against Coca-Cola, explaining the effect of caffeine on the human body. "I consider caffeine a habit-forming drug," said the former president of the American Medical Association. "It creates a desire to repeat the dose."

Others described how caffeine caused digestion ailments and heart failure. A professor of pharmacology at Harvard said that eight glasses of Coca-Cola contained enough caffeine to a kill a 160-pound man.

After the experts' testimony, Coca-Cola's lawyer asked the judge to dismiss the case. The attorney argued that nothing extra, specifically caffeine, had been added to the drink's formula. All the ingredients in the formula made Coca-Cola the unique, well-known beverage it was. Therefore, there was no basis for the charge of adulteration or misbranding.

The judge agreed and dismissed the case.

The government appealed the decision to a higher court. After several years of legal wrangling, Coca-Cola reduced the caffeine in its formula, but didn't remove it.

It was another disappointment for Wiley. He was convinced that caffeine in the soft drink was a health threat. "It will not be long before a milk dealer will discover that by adding a grain or two of caffeine to his milk it will become more popular . . . ," he wrote his friend Norman Hapgood, *Collier's* editor, "and soon we will have our bread and our meat treated in the same way. It will open wide the flood gates to drug addiction in our foods."

The 1910 advertisement promotes Coca-Cola as the perfect summer drink: "It's a liquid breeze."

This newspaper advertisement from June 21, 1912, mentions Coca-Cola's "vindication" at the Chattanooga trial.

DEPARTURE

By early 1912, Wiley was frustrated. Secretary Wilson and both Presidents Roosevelt and Taft had stripped away his ability to enforce the Food and Drugs Act. Wiley considered these men more sympathetic to the food manufacturers than to the public.

When a popular woman's magazine, *Good Housekeeping*, offered to double his salary, he listened. He had a family to think about now. His wife was pregnant with their first child.

Besides being an editor at *Good Housekeeping*, Wiley would have his own laboratory to test foods and drugs. He decided he could accomplish more as a private citizen than he could in government. It was time to leave the Bureau of Chemistry.

On March 15, 1912, he walked into Secretary Wilson's office and announced that he was quitting. Determined to publicize the reasons for his decision, Wiley sent his resignation letter to the press. Newspapers across the country printed it.

Wiley didn't hold back his criticisms. Despite the efforts of the Bureau of Chemistry, he complained, neither the Roosevelt nor Taft administrations enforced the law. "I saw the fundamental principles of the Food and Drugs Act, as they appeared to me, one by one paralyzed or discredited." He went on to write that he had been "left to come into daily contact with the men who secretly planned my destruction."

Harvey Wiley had led the Bureau for twenty-nine years. He later said of his time in the Department of Agriculture: "I was in the midst of a continual fight from the beginning to end; but always I did what I thought was right, forged ahead and usually won."

Wiley had lost key battles during his final five years as the Bureau's chief. But the government agency he took over in 1883 would one day grow to a level Wiley never imagined.

Harvey Wiley led the Bureau of Chemistry from 1883 to 1912. He considered himself a scientist, not a government bureaucrat.

ANNA CAMPBELL KELTON (1877–1964) in 1898, age twenty-one. Harvey Wiley first met his future wife when she worked for two years as his secretary at the Division of Chemistry. He proposed marriage. Thinking he was too old for her, Anna turned him down and took a job at the Library of Congress. Wiley carried this photograph in his watch for ten years until she finally accepted his proposal. They married on February 27, 1911, when he was sixty-six and she was thirty-three, spending their honeymoon at the Coca-Cola trial in Tennessee. A leader in women's organizations, Anna was as dedicated to the pure-food movement as Wiley.

Harvey and Anna Wiley pose in their home, about 1912, after he became an editor at *Good Housekeeping*.

Anna, second from left, was active in the Federation of Women's Clubs and the suffrage movement. This photo is from 1914 when she and other women visited the White House. Upon her marriage, one of her friends from the Woman Suffrage Association sent her a congratulatory note: "I know that you are not going to give up your principles for him or any other man." Anna didn't. In November 1917, she was arrested with other women from the National Woman's Party when they picketed the White House in the call for voting rights. The banner she carried read "Mr. President how long must women wait for liberty?" Harvey Wiley was supportive of his wife's activities, serving as the first president of the Men's League for Woman Suffrage.

In this 1916 family photo, Anna poses with the boys.

Harvey and Anna Wiley had two sons, Harvey Jr., born 1912 (shown here), and John, born 1914. When Harvey Jr. was born, reporters labeled him the Pure Food Baby.

CHAPTER SEVEN

OLD BORAX

"Science fails of its purpose which does not have
in view the welfare and happiness of man."
—Harvey Wiley

The public reaction to Wiley's resignation was mixed.

The *Buffalo* [NY] *Courier*'s headline read: "Women Weep as 'Watchdog of the Kitchen' Quits After 29 Years."

Many in the press criticized the Department of Agriculture and how it had operated against Wiley. *Collier's Weekly* charged: "The Department is badly organized, full of incompetence, subject to political influence, unwilling to enforce the Pure Food Law, extravagant, reluctant to remedy evils." The magazine called for Secretary Wilson's firing.

> **Women Weep as "Watchdog of the Kitchen" Quits After 29 Years**
>
> Headline from the *Buffalo Courier*, March 16, 1912

Other newspapers disagreed. The *Salt Lake* [UT] *Herald-Republican* said of Wiley: "He was the cause of constant friction in the Department and it is perhaps just as well that he has retired."

Wiley's longtime ally Alice Lakey wrote to President Taft. Wiley's resignation was, she said, the "most serious blow that has fallen on pure-food legislation."

Wiley prized this cartoon
that appeared in the
Washington [DC] *Star* on
March 17, 1912, after he
resigned from the Bureau
of Chemistry.

Taft apparently wasn't sorry that Wiley resigned. He wrote in a private letter that, although Wiley was a "very earnest prosecutor of those whom he regarded as guilty of violating the Pure Food act," his actions had been "a constant source of dissension and lack of harmony."

CHANGING SIDES

Wiley never got over his negative feelings about Theodore Roosevelt. It annoyed him that the man received credit for the Food and Drugs Act. When Roosevelt ran for president again in 1912, this time on the third-party

Bull Moose ticket, his backers claimed he'd been an enthusiastic supporter of the food law. As Wiley and the other hardworking advocates saw it, Roosevelt didn't push the bill in Congress until very late in the game.

In Wiley's opinion, neither Roosevelt nor Taft did enough to ensure the law's enforcement. During the presidential race of 1912, lifelong Republican Harvey Wiley turned against Taft, who was running for his second term. Instead, Wiley supported Democrat Woodrow Wilson, who pledged to enforce the Act.

Paying his own expenses, Wiley campaigned for Wilson. In a speech in Indiana a month before the election, Wiley told an audience, "I am naturally not greatly enthused with the prospect of the continuation of this crime against humanity by the return of Theodore Roosevelt to supreme power."

He was just as critical of Taft. "By their fruits (not promises) shall ye know them. And these fruits have been scabby, worm-eaten, and rotten at the core."

After Wilson won the election and became president, he didn't follow through on his pledge. Wiley was disgusted.

WILEY'S ADVICE

Now out of government, Wiley was much happier serving as the director of the *Good Housekeeping* Bureau of Foods, Sanitation, and Health. "In this favorable environment," he wrote in 1916, "I have had unrestricted opportunity to carry on my battle for pure food, finding no enemy to stab me in the back."

His laboratory analyzed the chemical

DR. WILEY HAS RESIGNED!

A March 1912 cartoon from the *Louisville* [KY] *Post* depicts a celebration by chemical additives and quack drug makers after Wiley left government.

makeup of foods, beverages, proprietary medicines, and cosmetics. He used the results to rate these products based on their quality and safety. Could the ingredients do what the manufacturer claimed in its advertising? Wiley refused to allow advertisements for a tested item unless it had passed analyses showing it was "free from injurious substances." Products earning that endorsement joined other household items given the Seal of Approval by *Good Housekeeping.*

In his monthly columns, Wiley directed his advice to America's women, whom he knew made most of the decisions about food and drugs in their homes. He discussed overuse and addiction to drugs: "The drugs are not necessarily opium, morphin, or cocain, but they are very apt to be alcohol, caffein, and other deleterious or habit-forming materials. We are anxious to stop the habit of 'taking something' which is so peculiarly American."

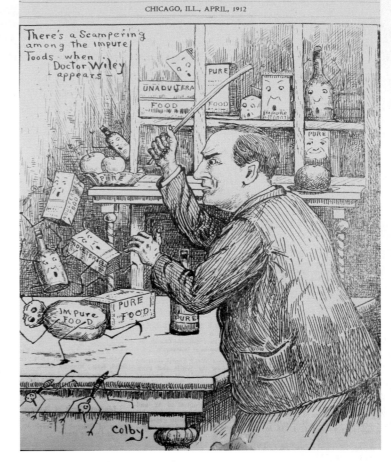

An April 1912 journal cover shows Wiley continuing to fight adulterated food and drugs. The caption reads: "Dr. Harvey W. Wiley, as a member of the Redpath family, is now going after adulterated foods, unhampered." The journal was published by an organization that sponsored some of Wiley's speeches.

Wiley warned women about the cosmetics advertised to do wonders for the complexion or hair. "Few of them are harmful," he wrote, "but they are all useless and extravagant and make impossible claims." One product supposedly made eyelashes and eyebrows grow longer. His *Good Housekeeping* lab found that it consisted of Vaseline mixed with fragrant citrus oil. "One dollar an ounce is rather high for [V]aseline," he quipped.

Wiley also continued his crusade for a healthy lifestyle. "Almost all Americans who can afford it overeat," he said in an interview. "We are extremists in our eating, starving, smoking, drinking, playing, working. And as a nation we are suffering from this, and shall, if we do not learn wisdom, suffer more."

Although his *Good Housekeeping* laboratories didn't test tobacco products for safety, Wiley had strong views about smoking based on his observations as a trained physician. In 1924, he warned his readers that tobacco promoted cancer and that more women would develop the disease if they smoked as much as men.

As deaths from lung cancer skyrocketed in the following decades, scientific evidence convinced others, too. In 1952, long after Wiley's death, *Good Housekeeping* stopped accepting cigarette ads. Not until 1964 did the U.S. Surgeon General issue an official report on the dangers of smoking.

REVENGE BY PEN

Though in his eighties, Wiley had no plans to retire from *Good Housekeeping*. He walked two miles to his office and worked at least twelve hours a day. In addition to his responsibilities at the magazine, Wiley gave lectures around the country about health and diet. "Work never killed anyone," he told a reporter. "Rusting out, however, kills hundreds of thousands."

In 1929, at age eighty-four, Wiley published *The History of a Crime Against the Food Law*. He bitterly detailed how his opponents in the Department of Agriculture and Congress sabotaged the 1906 law. Over the years, most companies had changed their production methods to avoid controversial chemicals. Formaldehyde, salicylic acid, and borax were no longer used as preservatives. Wiley was distressed that sodium benzoate was still allowed.

He wanted saccharin banned, too. The Department of Agriculture had stopped its use as a sugar substitute in manufacturing because it lacked food value—not because it was harmful. Saccharin remained available to consumers who chose to add it themselves. During the sugar shortages of World War I, the government lifted the ban against saccharin in processed foods.

In his book, Wiley faulted every president since Theodore Roosevelt for giving in to the same business groups that tried to prevent passage of the 1906 Act. "If the Bureau of Chemistry had been permitted to enforce the law

On June 30, 1926, the anniversary of the Pure Food and Drugs Law, Wiley (right) celebrates in New York City with Alice Lakey. The cake's creator stands on the left. Circling the bottom layer are eighty-two candles representing Wiley's age in 1926. On the top layer are twenty candles for the law's age. One large decorative candle rises above the rest.

as it was written . . . ," he said, "our foods and drugs would be wholly without any form of adulteration and misbranding. The health of our people would be vastly improved and their life greatly extended."

Wiley continued his activities at *Good Housekeeping* until the week before his eighty-fifth birthday in October 1929. Then he fell seriously ill from complications of a bad cold. That didn't stop him from finishing his autobiography in the months that followed. In it, he wrote that he did not yet consider himself retired.

But his health had deteriorated.

Throughout his life, Wiley had always known what he wanted and worked tirelessly to accomplish it. He felt the same way about death. "If I had my way about it," he wrote in his final year, "I would choose [to die] just

one minute before midnight so that I could put in a full day's work my last day on earth . . . . If I had any choice about the matter I would prefer to die of a heart attack, or of apoplexy, and to die instantly."

He almost got his wish.

Early on the morning of June 30, 1930, at his home in Washington, Harvey Wiley's heart gave out. It was the twenty-fourth anniversary of the signing of the Food and Drugs Act. Old Borax was gone.

As his family and many friends from his government years gathered around, Wiley was buried in Arlington National Cemetery while a bugler played taps. Engraved on his headstone, under his name, is "Father of the Pure Food Law."

Tributes spoke of his dedication to the cause of unadulterated food. "As a result of his labors," said a *Washington Post* editorial, "the span of life of the American people has been lengthened and their well-being enhanced."

His former assistant in the Poison Squad experiments, W. D. Bigelow, wrote: "He served the public not only by doing the thing that obviously had to be done, but also by helping the public to realize the further things that should be done."

Harvey Wiley, near the end of his life. He died on June 30, 1930, the anniversary of the signing of the Food and Drugs Act.

CHAPTER EIGHT

RADIOACTIVE MIRACLES

"Thousands of people have been positively and permanently relieved from innumerable disorders by the use of RADIUM."
—Advertisement for Radium Bath Compound, 1923

WALTER CAMPBELL (1877–1963) at his Department of Agriculture desk in 1923. Trained as a lawyer, Campbell joined the Bureau of Chemistry as chief inspector in 1907. He served as head of what is now the Food and Drug Administration from 1921 to 1924 and from 1927 until his retirement in 1944.

Harvey Wiley blamed government officials for not enforcing the Food and Drugs Act. Others saw defects in the law itself. Even before Wiley died, lawmakers attempted to fix it. Beginning in 1912, Congress passed several amendments to the Act, setting stricter rules about packaged foods and proprietary medicines.

In 1927, Congress shifted enforcement of the 1906 Act to a new division in the Department of Agriculture called the Food, Drug, and Insecticide Administration. In 1930, the name was changed to what we call it today—the U.S. Food and Drug Administration (FDA). Acting as its chief was Walter Campbell, the Kentucky lawyer whom Wiley hired as head inspector in 1907.

FAKE JAM

As Campbell was well aware, the amendments weren't enough to solve the law's problems. Although fewer food manufacturers were using the preservatives Wiley had condemned, scammers and cheats found ways to get around the rules. Companies didn't have to ask the FDA for its approval before selling a new food or drug. It was up to the government to catch abuses and take action.

Bred Spred was one example of the law's weaknesses. Designed to look like a high-quality jam, Bred Spred came in a glass jar with fruit pictured on the label. To the consumer, it appeared to be genuine jam. It wasn't. The product inside the jar contained color and flavoring but little, if any, fruit.

In the late 1920s and early 1930s, the FDA tried to stop Bred Spred's sale on the grounds that it was a cheap imitation of real jam. Yet the agency lost in court because Bred Spred's name and label didn't say that it was jam. The label didn't lie and was, therefore, legal.

Another shortcoming of the 1906 Act was that it didn't end the marketing of dangerous and useless drugs. A 1914 law required a doctor's prescription for drugs containing cocaine, opium, morphine, heroin, or codeine above

The Bred Spred jar looked as if it contained strawberry jam, but the product was a misleading imitation with few, if any, strawberries. In court, the FDA unsuccessfully tried to stop its sale under the 1906 Act. The agency also failed to end the deceptive labeling of this vinegar lookalike and the peanut spread containing scant peanuts. All three products remained on the market because they had distinctive names and didn't claim on the label to be the real thing.

Chemists analyze beverages in a Bureau of Chemistry laboratory, around 1920. In 1930, after several reorganizations within the Department of Agriculture, a new division called the Food and Drug Administration was made responsible for enforcing the 1906 Act.

a minimum amount. This cut down on addictive substances in quack medicines, but some companies continued to include them at low levels.

The proprietary drug companies were still allowed to *advertise* deceptive health claims for their nostrums. Sales were only restricted if the *label* claimed to cure ailments it could not cure. The development of radio gave companies a new way to advertise widely in addition to newspapers and magazines.

GOOD VIBRATIONS

By the 1920s, new chemicals were on the scene. Companies used them in proprietary medicines as well as in cosmetics, which hadn't been included in the 1906 Act. Doctors raised the alarm about the serious side effects they saw in patients who bought these products, reporting their concerns to their national organization, the American Medical Association (AMA).

The AMA set up a laboratory to analyze products that might cause addiction or harm. The lab also looked into medical devices advertised to diagnose and treat disease. Like cosmetics, these devices weren't regulated by the 1906 Act. The test results appeared in pamphlets and in the weekly *Journal of the American Medical Association.*

In the early 1920s, a machine named the Oscilloclast claimed to cure all known illnesses by producing electric pulses that matched the vibrations of diseased cells. When the patient was attached to the Oscilloclast by wires, the pulses supposedly demolished the disease.

Ironically, the man whose novel helped push the Food and Drugs Act through Congress, Upton Sinclair, was convinced of the Oscilloclast's powers. He wrote a magazine article in 1922, praising its inventor, Dr. Albert Abrams. "He will take rank in future times," wrote Sinclair, "among the

The Oscilloclast looked impressive, but it was a worthless fraud.

greatest benefactors of the human race . . . I pay to this great scientist the tribute of my love and admiration."

The AMA, physicians, and numerous scientists saw the Oscilloclast for what it was—a fraud. But the FDA lacked the legal authority to stop its sale.

THE DIAL PAINTERS

In 1898, physicists Marie and Pierre Curie discovered the element radium, for which they won the 1903 Nobel Prize in Physics. By the early 1900s, doctors realized that radium could destroy cancer cells. They also used it—either injected or in pill form—to treat everything from hair loss to high blood pressure.

Companies put radium into beverages, cosmetics such as lipstick and powder, and even toothpaste and candy. Advertisements hailed it as the cure for almost any affliction. "If you are sick," touted one ad, "don't get discouraged until you have tried this new and reasonably priced treatment."

Radium soda and water offered the consumer vim and vigor. Radium creams made skin look younger. Radium soaps took away pain. Health spas promoted their radioactive hot springs as healing havens.

Radium tablets, creams, and soaps were guaranteed to make the user look and feel younger. Radium bath powders claimed to cure nerve ailments and rheumatism. Many of these products were fake, containing no radium or too little to be harmful.

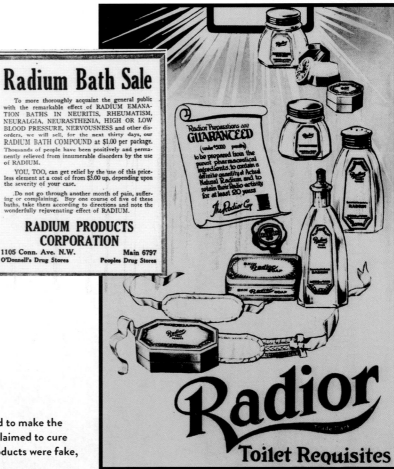

Glandular Balance

The fountain of perpetual youth has not yet been discovered, but it is conceded by eminent authorities that a balanced glandular system will give a longer lease on life and maintain a more youthful appearance and vitality while one does live.

Radium Tonic Tablets

—composed of gland extracts and Radium, the two greatest gland restoratives known, have restored health, energy and vitality to hundreds of men and women.

If you need a good tonic or general building up, try a few boxes of these remarkable TABLETS.

When ordering state whether for men or women.

At All Leading Drug Stores

Radium Bath Sale

To more thoroughly acquaint the general public with the remarkable effect of RADIUM EMANATION BATHS IN NEURITIS, RHEUMATISM, NEURALGIA, NEURASTHENIA, HIGH OR LOW BLOOD PRESSURE, NERVOUSNESS and other disorders, we will sell, for the next thirty days, our RADIUM BATH COMPOUND at $1.00 per package. Thousands of people have been positively and permanently relieved from innumerable disorders by the use of RADIUM.

YOU, TOO, can get relief by the use of this priceless element at a cost of from $5.00 up, depending upon the severity of your case.

Do not go through another month of pain, suffering or complaining. Buy one course of five of these baths, take them according to directions and note the wonderfully rejuvenating effect of RADIUM.

RADIUM PRODUCTS CORPORATION

1105 Conn. Ave. N.W.   Main 6797
O'Donnell's Drug Stores   Peoples Drug Stores

Radior Preparations are GUARANTEED (under $5000 penalty) to be prepared from the purest pharmaceutical ingredients to contain a definite quantity of Actual Natural Radium and to retain their Radio-activity for at least 20 years

The Radior Co

Radior Toilet Requisites

During World War I, a company in Orange, New Jersey, called U.S. Radium Corporation began producing wristwatches that shined in the dark. A combination of radium and a zinc chemical produced the dial's green glow.

Using this mixture, young female factory workers hand-painted numbers on the watch faces. Each worker painted more than two hundred watch dials a day, constantly pinching the brush tip with her lips to sharpen it . . . and ingesting radium each time.

The young women weren't careful with the paint. They colored their fingernails and skin with it. And why not? Radium was all the rage as the miracle chemical that made you look good and feel energetic.

But magical radium turned out to be a killer that stayed in their bodies

Young women paint watch dials with radium at the U.S. Radium Corporation in New Jersey, around 1922.

forever. Within a few years, the dial painters were sick. They developed sores in their mouths. Their jawbones disintegrated. Their legs and hips broke. Instead of becoming energized, their bodies weakened. Though only in their twenties, nine of them had died by 1924.

Curious scientists investigated. They found that the bones of one victim were radioactive. The breath of still-living dial painters contained radon, a gas produced when radium breaks down. Radium dust filled the air at the watch factory, covering surfaces.

Eventually, scientists learned that the human body stores radium in the skeleton. Radiation from the chemical destroys the bones and leads to anemia and exhaustion.

WONDER DRUG

By 1925, radium's shining reputation had been tarnished. The Bureau of Chemistry (soon to be the FDA) put out warnings about radium remedies, and most physicians recognized the danger. Yet the quack medicine companies continued to sell harmful products to gullible customers looking for a magic cure. The 1906 law didn't give the Bureau the power to stop their sale.

Unlike some quack radium products, Radithor contained dangerous radioactive water.

One of these nostrums was Radithor, which promised to work wonders on the ailing body. Eben Byers believed the promises. A well-educated, middle-aged businessman and amateur golfer, he started using Radithor in 1928 following a painful arm injury. Byers drank at least a two-ounce bottle of Radithor every day. At first, it made him feel invigorated. But the feeling didn't last.

By the time Byers connected his headaches and anemia to Radithor, it was too late. He became emaciated. His kidneys failed. His teeth fell out. His bones crumbled. After Byers died at age fifty-one in March 1932, an autopsy revealed that his body had been destroyed exactly like the dial painters'.

By some estimates, he had received the same amount of radiation as thousands of X-rays—far more than a lethal amount. His bones were so "strongly radioactive" that he had to be buried in a lead casket to prevent the escape of hazardous radiation.

Byers's death made headlines. The *New York Times*'s front page announced: "Eben M. Byers Dies of Radium Poisoning: Noted Sportsman, 51, Had Drunk a Patented Water for a Long Period." One newspaper editorial demanded, "Is the Federal Food and Drugs Act, then, a joke?"

In many ways, it was. Physicians and scientists knew that radium was "detrimental to health and fatal to life." But under the 1906 Act, the FDA could do nothing against Radithor or other dangerous drugs except warn the public.

Radithor's label truthfully said that it contained radium. The law didn't require manufacturers to put warnings on medicine labels. The company made its false health claims in its advertising, not on the product label. That was legal, too.

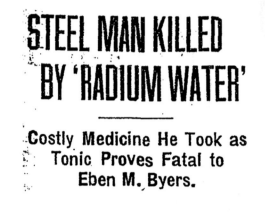

STEEL MAN KILLED BY 'RADIUM WATER'

Costly Medicine He Took as Tonic Proves Fatal to Eben M. Byers.

Headline in the *Washington Post*, April 1, 1932, announces Byers's death by radium poisoning.

It took another government agency to force deadly Radithor off the market. The Federal Trade Commission had the authority to charge the manufacturer with false advertising claims. The company voluntarily stopped making Radithor and escaped punishment.

ALLURING LASHES

Since 1906, many new cosmetics had been introduced to consumers. Like proprietary medicines, these were advertised in magazines and newspapers. Women swore by them.

In May 1933, Mrs. Brown (an alias used by the FDA to protect her identity) went to her beauty shop to have her hair cut and set. That evening was a special occasion. She was to be honored by the local Parent-Teacher Association for her work as its secretary.

The beautician suggested to Mrs. Brown that dyeing her eyebrows and eyelashes would make her look even better. Mrs. Brown agreed, and the beautician used Lash Lure, a dye that was the latest fashion at beauty parlors. The advertisements claimed that a Lash Lure woman "Radiates Personality."

Within two hours of her Lash Lure treatment, Mrs. Brown's eyes began burning and watering. Soon they were swollen shut and she could barely see. By the next morning, her entire face was swollen. For the next several months, Mrs. Brown was bedridden in extreme pain. Her eyeballs had been destroyed, and she would never see again.

This woman's eyelashes and eyebrows were dyed with Lash Lure at a beauty salon in May 1933. The second photograph was taken a month later showing her damaged eyeballs. The FDA produced this poster to publicize the dangers of the cosmetic.

A year later, an unsuspecting Florida woman used Lash Lure, too. She had the same reaction. Unlike Mrs. Brown, she died after eight days.

Doctors reported other cases to the *Journal of the American Medical Association*. One woman ended up with her eyes swollen shut and draining pus. She didn't recover for six weeks. Another woman landed in the hospital with painful eyes the day after having her eyelashes and eyebrows dyed. After two weeks of treatments with compresses, she felt well enough to go home. Her vision didn't return to normal for a month.

Researchers discovered that a chemical in the Lash Lure dye, para-phenylenediamine, had caused the damage. But the FDA had no power to stop the sale of cosmetics containing the dangerous dye. Lash Lure stayed available in beauty shops across the country, continuing to cause injury.

KOREMLU

During the 1930s, the maker of Koremlu advertised the hair-removing cream in the top women's magazines. The product certainly worked, and it was popular. In one year, women bought one hundred twenty thousand jars in department stores alone.

The advertising claimed the cream was safe to use. Customers didn't know that Koremlu was made from thallium, one of the most potent poisons. The label wasn't legally required to mention that important detail. The medical community had known that thallium was deadly since the late 1800s. In fact, it was sold as rat poison in the early 1920s.

Koremlu first went on sale in spring 1930. Within months, the *Journal of the American Medical Association* reported that women had had frightening reactions after using it to remove facial, leg, and armpit hair. They suffered blurred vision and painful, weak legs and feet. They lost their scalp hair, even though they hadn't applied the cream there. Some victims gradually recovered after they stopped using the cream. For others, the damage was permanent.

One distraught woman wrote First Lady Eleanor Roosevelt: "I started losing my eyesight . . . Every doctor I go to tells me the same thing I have Retrobulbur Neuritis with Optic Nerve Atrophy for which there is no cure

. . . [Koremlu Cream] took from me all I had that made life worth while
My eyes."

Some states and cities banned the sale of Koremlu. The FDA sent out
public warnings about the product. But without authority to ban hazardous
cosmetics, the agency could not order Koremlu off the national market.

Even when people died or were sickened,
lawsuits against these companies only
stopped the owners temporarily. They
started new businesses and were soon
raking in the profits again.

100,000,000 GUINEA PIGS

In 1933, two members of a consumer
protection organization wrote a book called
100,000,000 Guinea Pigs. Arthur Kallet
and F. J. Schlink claimed that Americans
(the population in the 1930 census was 123
million) were guinea pigs for the chemical
industry, and the government wasn't
stopping it.

The Listerine advertisement appeared in *Country Gentleman*
magazine in November 1930. At that time, the Listerine company
marketed mouthwash, shaving cream, and dandruff shampoo. In
1933, *100,000,000 Guinea Pigs* criticized Listerine for claiming
that its mouthwash prevented colds and sore throats. In the late
1970s, the Federal Trade Commission, the agency in charge of
advertising, forced Listerine to stop making this claim because no
evidence supported it.

The authors revealed examples of
dangerous foods, drugs, and cosmetics sold
in the United States. Echoing Harvey Wiley's
complaint, they charged that the government
failed to regulate products like Radithor,
Koremlu, and Lash Lure because of pressure from manufacturers and
politicians. Sometimes the ill effects didn't show up for years. By then,
millions of people had used the product.

Kallet and Schlink suggested that an increase in cancer cases
since 1930 was due to chemicals in food and drugs. They wrote that
"it is exceedingly likely that the poisons" would damage the kidneys,
stomach, and intestines and lower resistance to diseases, shortening life
expectancy in some cases by "several decades."

The 1906 Act made it illegal for the label on proprietary medicines to include fraudulent claims. The quack drug companies did their lying, instead, on postcards, magazines, newspapers, and store signs (like this poster).

The book called out well-known brands as unsafe or ineffective. According to the authors, the amount of potassium chlorate in a tube of Pebeco toothpaste could kill three people.

They accused Listerine's manufacturer of deceptively promoting the mouthwash as a cold and sore throat preventative. The company's advertising proclaimed, "The moment it enters the mouth, it kills millions of germs." Kallet and Schlink described bacteriologists' tests proving that Listerine didn't kill many of the most common microbes.

100,000,000 Guinea Pigs became a bestseller. People were appalled by what they read. They hadn't realized that companies were still selling nostrums and cosmetics with ingredients known by scientists and doctors to be harmful. Many consumers assumed that the 1906 Food and Drugs Act had stopped that.

The book criticized the government for its inaction. But the FDA's leader, Walter Campbell, knew that his hands were tied by the limits of the 1906 Act. He was grateful for any help he could get to fix the law and strengthen the FDA. "If this muck-raking publication furthers these ends," he told a friend, "it will not have been published in vain."

CHAPTER NINE

RASPBERRY COUGH SYRUP

"It is time to make practical improvements."

—President Franklin Roosevelt

In 1933, Walter Campbell recommended that the original Food and Drugs Act be totally revised. The law had too many loopholes and no longer protected the American public from deception and danger. He and others at the Department of Agriculture helped to put a new bill before Congress.

THE CHAMBER OF HORRORS

When a Senate committee discussed a replacement for the 1906 Act, the FDA created a special informational display for the committee. Inspectors

People who believed advertisements by the quack drug companies often didn't visit a doctor for more effective help. Nostrums that promised to cure cancer gave false hope to the sick.

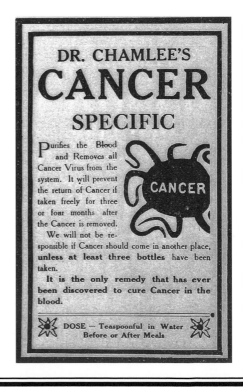

DR. CHAMLEE'S **CANCER** SPECIFIC

Purifies the Blood and Removes all Cancer Virus from the system. It will prevent the return of Cancer if taken freely for three or four months after the Cancer is removed.

We will not be responsible if Cancer should come in another place, **unless at least three bottles** have been taken.

It is the only remedy that has ever been discovered to cure Cancer in the blood.

DOSE — Teaspoonful in Water Before or After Meals

The woman holds a candy in one hand and, in the other, the same treat cracked open to reveal a toy ring. Children who ate the candy sometimes choked on the surprise toy or coin. These candies were part of the Chamber of Horrors exhibit set up at the Department of Agriculture. The FDA sent smaller versions of the exhibit around the country.

from around the country sent in examples of fraudulent and harmful products that the existing law did not control. The press nicknamed the exhibit the Chamber of Horrors.

The collection highlighted imitation foods, such as Bred Spred. It included candy with small toys hidden inside that children had choked on. X-rays showed a toy stuck in a child's throat. Though an obvious hazard, the FDA couldn't stop the candy's sale.

Jars and packages with false bottoms looked as if they held more food than they did. Under the 1906 Act, misleading packaging was legal.

Cosmetics hadn't been much of a concern in 1906. By the 1930s, it was a billion-dollar-a-year business. The FDA presented photographs and news articles about Lash Lure and Koremlu. Some tonics in the exhibit had caused fatalities, and death certificates were displayed as proof. A poster told the tragic story of Eben Byers and Radithor.

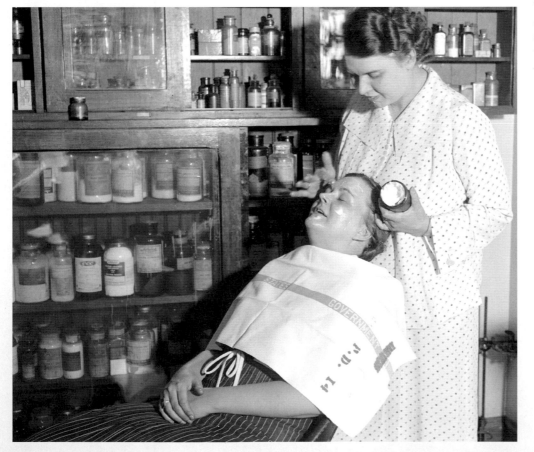

Testing cosmetic face creams for safety and effectiveness at the Department of Agriculture in 1937

One part of the Chamber of Horrors included a newspaper page filled with dozens of advertisements for products to treat or cure a range of ailments: diabetes, bronchitis, asthma, arthritis, high blood pressure, stomach ulcers, baldness. None of the products did what it claimed.

FRANKLIN (1882–1945) AND ELEANOR ROOSEVELT (1884–1962) in 1932, the year he was elected president. A victim of polio eleven years before, Franklin lost the use of his legs and wore leg braces. Here he supports himself with a cane and Eleanor's arm. The First Lady was a vocal supporter of a revised pure food and drug law.

Although many of the tonics and creams contained no harmful ingredients, they endangered health because customers used them instead of getting legitimate medical care.

After hearing about the Chamber of Horrors exhibit, First Lady Eleanor Roosevelt visited it. Later, she met fifty reporters in her office for a regular interview session.

"I have just been over to the department of agriculture," the First Lady said. From a folder, she pulled out the gruesome photograph of Mrs. Brown, the Lash Lure victim, and passed it around. "It is high time that this hoodwinking of women was stopped."

Mrs. Roosevelt mentioned the bill in Congress to replace the 1906 Act. "It should have the support of every woman in the country."

RODENT HAIRS AND FLY WINGS

President Franklin Roosevelt asked Congress to pass the new bill, too. In his written message to Congress in March 1935, he acknowledged the changes in products that had occurred since 1906. "The great majority of those engaged in the trade in food and drugs do not need regulation," he wrote. "Present legislation ought to be directed primarily toward a small minority of evaders and chiselers."

Opposition to the proposed bill came from the same groups that had been against the 1906 law: some food manufacturers, proprietary-medicine makers, and advertisers.

Supporters included consumer groups, women's clubs, the Woman's

Christian Temperance Union, the American Medical Association, parents' and teachers' organizations, and others who had fought for the original Wiley Act.

Even young people sent letters supporting the bill. One arrived for President Roosevelt from the ten-year-old daughter of Mrs. Brown: "My mother has been trying to put a new law across so that no more poison will be put in this dye . . . My mother is totally blind and we want you to please help us to get the law across."

To promote the bill's passage, the FDA's chief educational officer wrote a book in 1936 about the famous FDA exhibit. Author Ruth deForest Lamb called it *American Chamber of Horrors*. She dedicated her book to twenty-one women who led organizations agitating for the new law. One was Harvey Wiley's widow, Anna, who represented the District of Columbia Federation of Women's Clubs.

Besides discussing the Chamber of Horrors products, Lamb described other offenses that the FDA had uncovered in recent years. Inspectors were alarmed when they examined samples of butter that looked clean and edible. Further analysis showed: "Hay; fragments of chicken feathers; maggots; clumps of mold . . .; grasshoppers; straw chaff; beetles; cow, dog, cat and rodent hairs; moths; grass and other vegetable matter; cockroaches; dust; ants; fly legs; broken fly wings; metallic filings; remains of rats, mice and other animals."

In one pound of butter delivered to a candy factory, inspectors found enough maggots to reach nearly twelve feet if laid end to end.

Yet the eye-opening details in Lamb's book and the lobbying by FDA supporters didn't convince Congress to pass the new bill. The influence of its opponents was too great. Once again, it took a tragedy to change the minds of lawmakers.

TASTY ELIXIR

In the early 1930s, scientists discovered that a chemical called sulfanilamide healed streptococcal bacteria infections. It seemed to be a wonder drug that could cure many diseases.

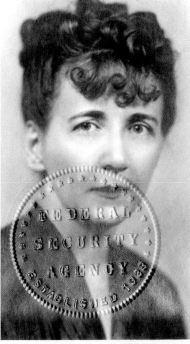

RUTH DE FOREST LAMB (1896–1978) graduated from Vassar College and worked in advertising before becoming the FDA's first chief educational officer, in 1933. This was her government ID when the FDA was part of the Federal Security Agency. Today, the FDA is an agency in the Department of Health and Human Services.

One of the several companies that had been producing the drug as a pill, S. E. Massengill Company of Tennessee, realized there was a market for a liquid form. The company's head chemist, Harold Watkins, took on the task of figuring out how to make it.

Because sulfanilamide didn't dissolve in water or alcohol, Watkins looked for another liquid that worked. He came up with a pink, sweet, raspberry-flavored concoction, which the company called Elixir Sulfanilamide. No one at Massengill tested the solution to see whether it might be harmful to humans. According to the Food and Drugs Act of 1906, that wasn't necessary.

In early fall 1937, the company shipped the new drug throughout the United States. The label on each bottle stated that the liquid contained the medicine sulfanilamide. It didn't list the other ingredients, nor did the law require that. Doctors were glad to have the drug in a form that children would willingly swallow.

A DEADLY ERROR

Within a month, the American Medical Association received a troubling report from Tulsa, Oklahoma. Six people had died from kidney failure after taking Elixir Sulfanilamide. The AMA alerted the Massengill Company that there was a problem with the new drug.

The company sent a thousand recall telegrams to physicians, druggists, and its two hundred salesmen. But the telegram didn't mention why the company was recalling the medicine. It was silent about the deaths.

Meanwhile, the AMA used radio and newspaper publicity to sound the warning to doctors and the public.

The FDA had already heard about the Oklahoma deaths from a New York doctor. Immediately, Walter Campbell assigned most of his chemists and inspectors to investigate. Working with local and state authorities, the FDA tracked down and took possession of the rest of the drug on the market within about a month. Fortunately, fewer than twelve gallons had landed in the hands of patients across the country.

The agency could do little else. The only law the Massengill Company had broken was mislabeling the new medicine. According to FDA rules, a product couldn't be called an elixir unless it contained alcohol, and Elixir Sulfanilamide contained none. The company paid a fine for misbranding the drug.

Researchers analyzed the drug and did tests on animals to identify the harmful ingredient. The culprit was diethylene glycol, the chemical Harold Watkins used to dissolve sulfanilamide. Three-quarters of Elixir Sulfanilamide was made of it, and it was deadly.

Useful in industry, diethylene glycol is chemically similar to the active ingredient in antifreeze. Two research studies had previously shown that the substance was lethal in rats at low concentrations. Watkins hadn't known about them.

Those few gallons of the toxic medicine reached 350 people in fifteen states. Most patients had been prescribed Elixir by their doctor for a variety of illnesses including sore throats and ear infections. The drug was fatal to 107 of them, including 34 children.

Before the victims painfully died from kidney failure, they suffered for as long as three weeks with nausea, abdominal cramps, and even convulsions. Other patients vomited when first taking the medicine and stopped dosing themselves. That saved their lives.

In January 1939, more than a year after the first patient swallowed Elixir Sulfanilamide, its inventor was found dead at his home from a self-inflicted gunshot. Harold Watkins's wife claimed he had been cleaning his gun when it went off accidentally. But many suspected that the chemist had committed suicide out of despair over his error.

Elixir Sulfanilamide contained diethylene glycol, a deadly chemical.

OUTRAGE

Just as the stomach-churning meat slaughterhouses had awakened the public, so did the Elixir Sulfanilamide tragedy. Children had died!

One devastated Oklahoma mother wrote to President Roosevelt about the death of her six-year-old daughter, Joan: "We can see her little body tossing to and fro and hear that little voice screaming with pain . . . It is my plea that you will take steps to prevent such sales of drugs that will take little lives."

ELIXIR DEATHS TOTAL FIFTY-ONE
Medical Association Raps Federal Laws

Headline from the October 27, 1937, *Los Angeles Times* before officials knew how many people had been affected. More than one hundred known deaths were eventually attributed to the medicine. The American Medical Association blamed inadequate food and drug laws for allowing Elixir Sulfanilamide to reach consumers.

Headlines called it a "Death Drug" and "Deadly 'Elixir.'" People insisted on protection from medicines that might kill their children. With voters outraged and reelection just months away, lawmakers listened. Congress finally passed the proposed bill to replace the 1906 law. On June 25, 1938, President Franklin Roosevelt signed the Food, Drug, and Cosmetic Act.

A STRONGER FDA

For the first time, cosmetics and medical devices were regulated. The FDA now had the power to seize ineffective or dangerous products.

Cosmetics ingredients had to be sanitary and harmless if used according to the label. But, except for some color additives, manufacturers didn't have to prove safety before selling a product. That was up to the FDA.

The agency stopped Koremlu sales because thallium was hazardous. It charged Lash Lure with adulteration because the cosmetic was dangerous when used according to instructions. Eyelash and eyebrow dyes containing para-phenylenediamine were prohibited. The FDA required a label on all hair dyes containing the chemical, warning against applying the product around the eyes.

The 1938 Act expanded food regulations, too, giving the FDA authority to set stricter standards of quality and package contents. Bred Spred was considered misbranded because it appeared to be a standard food—jam— without containing the ingredients set by FDA's rules. For jam, those contents included fruit.

The definition of adulteration now included bacteria, insect and rodent parts, and toxic chemicals. Colors used in food, drugs, and cosmetics had to be approved.

Consumer groups applauded these changes. "It makes a tremendous difference both in money and health to thousands of families, especially those of low income," said Helen Hall, chair of the Consumers National Federation. "It will not only protect them from impure or harmful products, but obviously they will get more in food value for the dollar spent in the market."

The 1938 law added new drug regulations. Medicine labels had to show the active ingredients and instructions for safe use. Consumers should be warned of situations when the medication might be dangerous. Any drug that was hazardous when used according to directions, such as Radithor, was banned.

Companies were required to show proof that a new drug was safe before the FDA permitted its sale. That rule could have prevented the Elixir Sulfanilamide tragedy.

Despite its improvements over the 1906 law, the Food, Drug, and Cosmetic Act had weaknesses. Although a company was supposed to notify the FDA when it wanted to sell a new drug, the agency had just sixty days to review the request. If the reviewer didn't decide in time, the drug was automatically approved and went on sale anyway.

That detail turned out to have horrifying consequences.

CHAPTER TEN

The WATCHDOGS

"In next to no time, the fighting over the new drug laws that had been going on for five or six years suddenly melted away."
—Frances Kelsey

In the 1950s, a German company developed a drug called thalidomide and sold it as a sleeping pill. Thalidomide also turned out to ease nausea in pregnant women. The company called the medicine "non-toxic" and "completely harmless even for infants." It was sold over the counter without a doctor's prescription.

To expand its market beyond Europe, the German manufacturer and its American partner asked the FDA to allow the drug's sale in the United States.

"TOO GLOWING"

In 1960, Dr. Frances Kelsey was hired by the FDA to review new drugs. After only a month in her new job, she was assigned the task of determining whether thalidomide should be approved to market.

Well-qualified and experienced, Kelsey had doctoral degrees in medicine and pharmacology. As a graduate student at the University of Chicago in 1937, she had been on the team of scientists that identified diethylene glycol as the deadly ingredient in Elixir Sulfanilamide.

After Kelsey reviewed the materials submitted by the German and American drug companies, she was "very unimpressed." She thought the testing of thalidomide was flawed and unscientific. She even wondered whether the results had been falsified. "The claims made . . . for thalidomide were too glowing," she said later.

The pressure from the drug companies to grant approval mounted, but Kelsey and others in the FDA insisted on getting more information about the tests. Each time the companies resubmitted their application with the additional facts, the sixty-day approval period restarted. Kelsey's requests for data about the medical effects of thalidomide delayed the drug's sale in the United States for months.

Then the shocking reports emerged from Europe. Babies had been born without arms and legs. Some infants had defects in their internal organs, including the heart and intestines. By 1961, it was clear that the babies' mothers had one thing in common. They had taken thalidomide

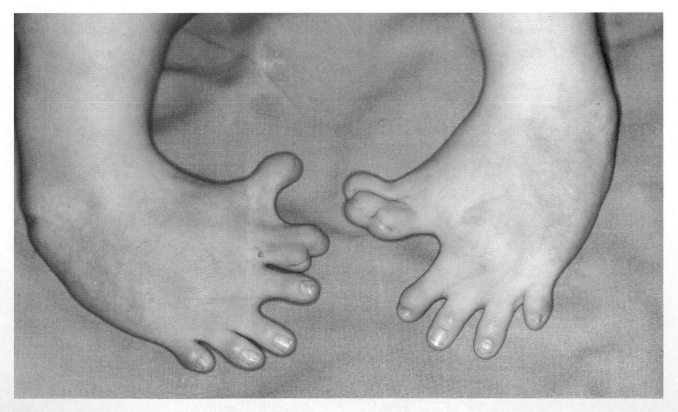

Thalidomide caused malformations, such as this victim's feet.

during pregnancy. The drug companies apparently suspected trouble earlier and never informed the FDA.

HEARTBREAKING

Because Kelsey and the FDA moved slowly in granting approval, thalidomide was never sold in the United States. Unfortunately, the companies had already been testing the drug on American mothers before asking for FDA permission to market it here. According to the 1938 Act, they were allowed to distribute the drug if it was part of an experiment. Doctors participating in the test had given thalidomide to pregnant women. None of the mothers had a clue about the risk.

Thalidomide had been sold in forty-six countries. At least eight thousand babies were born with serious abnormalities, most in Germany and the rest of Europe. Five to seven thousand more died before their birth from damage caused by the drug. These are estimates, however, and some experts think

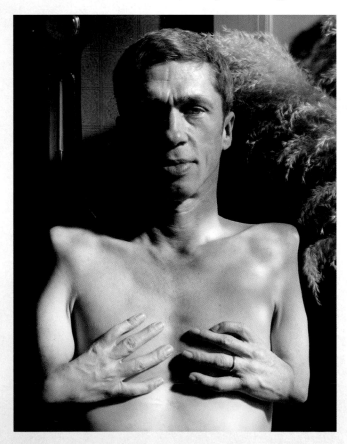

the numbers were much higher. In the United States, about twenty affected babies were born. Up to two dozen others died before birth.

Photographs of the deformed children appeared in newspapers and magazines. The images were heartbreaking, and the American public demanded action. Once again, a tragedy had revealed weaknesses in a law meant to protect the nation's health.

Concerns about drug safety had been simmering in Congress for several years. Yet a bill addressing the issue failed to make headway. The dramatic publicity about the thalidomide babies brought the issue to a boil.

In October 1962, Congress passed the Kefauver-Harris Amendments to the 1938

The mother of this British man, born in 1962, took thalidomide during her pregnancy. He is an actor and drummer.

Food, Drug, and Cosmetic Act, updating the procedure for drug approvals. Companies had to demonstrate that a drug was safe and effective by using a new standard of well-designed scientific studies. If a company knew of problems with the drug, it was obligated to inform the FDA. The sixty-day review limit was gone. A drug could not be marketed to the public until the FDA granted its approval.

RULES CHANGE

Today, the Food, Drug, and Cosmetic Act continues to guide the FDA. The 1962 Kefauver-Harris Amendments are among dozens of new laws passed since 1938 that are designed to close loopholes and increase the FDA's duties.

The agency now has strict guidelines for human testing. An investigation like Wiley's Poison Squads would have to be quite different.

To safeguard participants, a review board must okay the study. Animal experiments will likely be required first, and perhaps a human study won't be permitted at all. Subjects must be given details about the experiment and its risks, and they must be told that they have the option of not participating. The expectant mothers who took thalidomide never had this information.

DR. FRANCES KELSEY (1914–2015) wears the President's Award for Distinguished Federal Civilian Service after President John Kennedy (1917–1963) presented it to her at the 1962 ceremony. Kelsey's skepticism about thalidomide prevented its sale in the United States. Later, Kelsey said of the award, "This was really a team effort."

Unlike Wiley's experiments with only young male subjects, males and females of various ages and races are tested. Special rules protect children and pregnant women. Ideally, an experiment is designed to minimize bias, even if unintentional. There are control groups. Whenever possible, subjects and researchers don't know who is a control and who is receiving the test substance.

Researchers also look for long-term effects, something Wiley didn't do.

Will the drug or food additive cause cancer, gene damage, harm a developing baby?

EXPANDING . . .

When Harvey Wiley became head of the Division of Chemistry in 1883, he had fewer than a dozen people on his staff. After 135 years, more than seventeen thousand employees work at the FDA, which is part of the Department of Health and Human Services. A commissioner appointed by the president heads the agency. The FDA regulates products that make up a quarter of the money Americans spend each year. (See sidebar on page 120)

Besides prescription medicines for both humans and animals, the FDA oversees over-the-counter drugs like aspirin, cough syrups, sunscreen, and fluoride toothpaste.

It still doesn't approve new cosmetics for safety and effectiveness before they're sold. But the products aren't

William Carter, who once cooked for the Poison Squad, later studied pharmaceutical chemistry and worked in FDA laboratories. He retired after more than forty years at the agency.

The FDA is responsible for the safety and effectiveness of food, drugs, and medical devices used with animals.

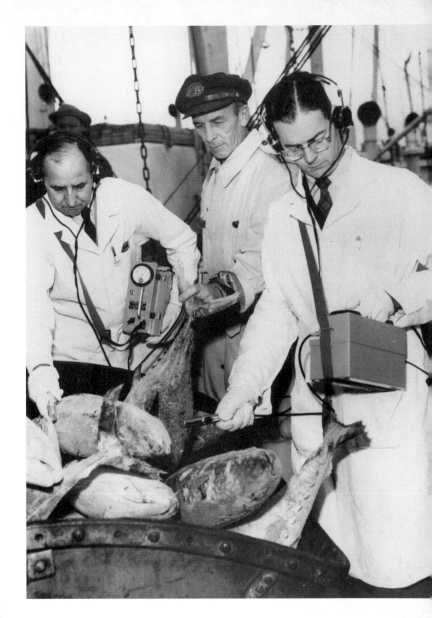

After nuclear bombs were tested in the atmosphere in the 1950s and 60s, FDA inspectors checked for unsafe levels of radiation in food, drugs, and cosmetics. In this photograph from about 1954, inspectors use a Geiger counter to measure the radioactivity of tuna that had been caught in the Pacific Ocean near the bomb-testing site. Today, the FDA's Center for Devices and Radiological Health is in charge of radiation safety.

allowed to include ingredients known to be unsanitary or harmful when used according to the label's directions. Some consumer advocates think cosmetics contain too many toxic chemicals and the FDA hasn't done enough to stop their use. They want Congress to pass a new law that requires the agency to evaluate the safety of these chemicals.

The FDA's responsibility for food safety has become more complicated than it was when Wiley focused on additives. Today's manufacturers no longer depend on large quantities of chemical preservatives. Modern methods of preserving and processing food include improved pasteurization, ultraviolet light, and electrical current. Researchers continue to pursue other approaches.

But other food hazards involve contamination by pesticides and by bacteria such as *Salmonella, Listeria,* and *E. coli* that cause foodborne illnesses. Each year, about forty-eight million Americans get sick from something they've eaten. That's more than one in seven people. To monitor these dangers, the FDA cooperates with the states and other federal agencies, particularly the Centers for Disease Control and Prevention

WHAT DOES THE FDA DO?

The U.S. Food and Drug Administration regulates products used every day by everybody. Congress has changed the agency's responsibilities several times since 1906. As of 2019, the FDA oversees:

★ Food (human and animal)

★ Drugs (human and animal; includes non-prescription drugs)

★ Dietary supplements (example: vitamins)

★ Biological products (examples: vaccines, blood)

★ Cosmetics (examples: shampoo, makeup, skin cream, deodorant, hair color)

★ Medical devices (examples: heart pacemakers, lasers, 3D printing of drugs and replacement body parts)

★ Radiation-emitting devices (examples: cell phones, microwave ovens)

★ Tobacco products

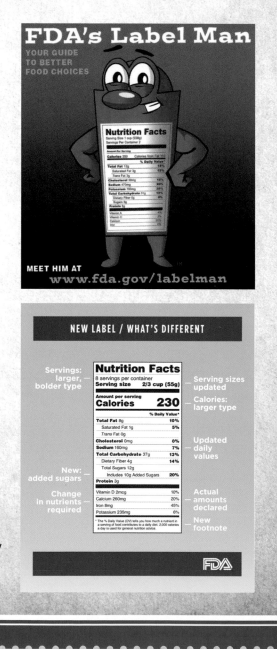

The FDA oversees nutritional labels on food, which include serving size, calories, and nutrient and vitamin content. Beginning in January 2020, food companies must replace existing labels (top) with new ones that are based on updated nutrition research (bottom). Larger serving sizes on the new labels better fit the amount people today actually eat.

(CDC), Environmental Protection Agency (EPA), and the U.S. Department of Agriculture (USDA).

Recent presidential administrations have proposed putting the oversight of food safety into a single agency—the USDA—leaving the FDA to focus on non-food issues, including drugs, cosmetics, and medical devices. Proponents of the change argue that this reorganization, by being more efficient, will better protect the nation's food. As of 2019, Congress has not approved this change.

FRAUDSTERS

Fraud continues, despite laws and regulations. Dishonest companies dilute beverages and add unapproved additives to food. They sell counterfeit products: a cheap fish species sold as an expensive one; inexpensive city tap water sold in a bottle as pricey mountain-spring water.

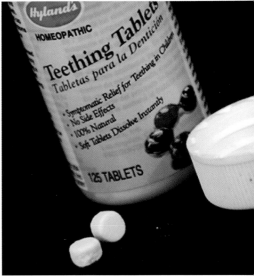

In 2017, Hyland's teething tablets were taken off the market by the manufacturer after an FDA warning about harmful levels of belladonna.

Some labels are misleading, such as bread identified as whole wheat when it contains corn flour. In fall 2019, the FDA warned a Massachusetts company to stop listing "love" as an ingredient in its granola. The product was misbranded because love doesn't qualify as a standard ingredient in granola . . . or in any other food.

Just as Wiley's first inspectors did in 1907, today's FDA inspectors search for these deceptions. They check facilities throughout the country that prepare foods and drugs. They also visit manufacturing plants in foreign countries that send products to the United States.

Inspectors find filthy factories contaminated by toxic chemicals, bugs, rats, and workers who wipe their noses while handling food. The FDA issues official public warnings about violations. If a company doesn't correct the problem immediately, the agency can seize products and stop their sale. Thousands of unsafe or fraudulent products are recalled each year after an FDA investigation.

Companies still try to entice consumers to buy worthless or harmful drugs. A century after Mrs. Winslow's Soothing Syrup endangered children, the FDA discovered a similar product on the market in 2016. A California company was illegally adding morphine to its non-prescription Licorice Coughing Liquid. The agency forced the company to recall the medicine.

A case from 2017 involved Hyland's Baby Teething Tablets, a non-prescription product sold online and in stores. The label claimed that the tablets eased infant discomfort in a "100% Natural" way with "No Side Effects." The FDA had not approved the product as safe or effective.

After receiving complaints from the public about children having bad reactions, the FDA investigated. Its chemists analyzed the tablets and found harmful levels of belladonna (also known as deadly nightshade). In certain doses, this toxic chemical can cause high heart rate, hallucinations, and seizures in young children. The agency issued safety alerts to warn parents.

In the wake of the FDA's formal request, the company recalled the tablets and stopped selling them in the United States. It continued to say on its website that the amount of belladonna was not dangerous. The tablets, it assured customers, "have been safely used by millions of children since being introduced to the U.S. market in 1945!"

To monitor contamination and nutrient levels in the food supply, the FDA regularly analyzes groceries typically bought by consumers.

GUARDING THE NATION'S HEALTH

A government agency with as much power as the FDA is certain to have critics.

Some of them point out that there are thousands of new drugs and food additives and the FDA can't possibly check the safety of all. They believe that the agency is too quick in giving the green light to new products and is too slow in recalling harmful ones. As a result, the public is at risk.

Other critics charge that the FDA is too big and controlling and wastes taxpayer money. They object to the government preventing people from making their own decisions. Some detractors say the FDA takes too long to approve new drugs and vaccines that could help people. And others accuse the agency of being too tough on businesses when it does inspections and issues recalls.

Dr. Harvey Washington Wiley, Father of the FDA

Harvey Wiley heard similar complaints about his Bureau of Chemistry in the early twentieth century. But Old Borax kept up his fight "toward improving the nutrition, and consequently the health of the nation."

After more than a hundred years, the results of his Poison Squad experiments have been questioned. Some of the chemicals he called toxic are safely added to food today. His understanding of the effects of preservatives on digestion was incomplete. Science advanced, and discoveries in nutrition and chemistry expanded our knowledge.

Yet Wiley started a tradition of using scientific research to determine the safety and effectiveness of food and drugs. Current laws reflect his view: chemicals should only be added when necessary; they should be labeled for the consumer; and manufacturers should prove a substance's safety before being permitted to add it.

A few months before his death, Wiley looked back on his life with satisfaction. He knew he had helped lay the foundation for the 1906 Food and Drugs Act. "Certainly it is important," he wrote of the day the law was signed, "in that long and proud record of legislation seeking to guard the well-being of men, women and children."

THE POISON SQUAD CHEMICALS

O f the chemical additives Wiley tested in his Poison Squad experiments, four are banned from food today: formaldehyde, borax, boric acid, and salicylic acid. The others (sulfites and sulfurous acid, benzoic acid and sodium benzoate, copper sulfate, and saltpeter) are allowed in certain foods in the smallest amount necessary. Caffeine and saccharin, two other additives to which Wiley objected, are commonly used.

The FDA has compiled a list of food additives believed to be safe, called GRAS ("generally recognized as safe"). Manufacturers are free to put these in their products. A substance can be removed from the list if new scientific evidence emerges. A company is supposed to get FDA approval before using a new additive that hasn't previously been permitted.

benzoic acid/sodium benzoate: Control bacteria growth. Used as preservatives. Today, **ALLOWED** in food in limited amounts.

borax/boric acid: Stop decay. Once used to preserve meat, fish, and butter and to mask the odor of spoilage. Both cause physical damage when taken internally. **NOT ALLOWED IN FOOD.** Today, boric acid is used as antiseptic, acne treatment, and cockroach killer. Borax makes up scouring powder and laundry detergent.

caffeine: ALLOWED to be added to soft drinks and as a stimulant to prescription and over-the-counter drugs.

copper sulfate: Kills bacteria, fungi, and algae. Once added to canned vegetables to make them greener and to disguise an inferior product. Today, copper is known to be an essential dietary element. **ALLOWED** in food in limited amounts.

formaldehyde: Kills microbes. Once added to dairy products and meat as a preservative. Known to trigger allergic reactions and cause cancer. **NOT ALLOWED IN HUMAN FOOD.** Used in hair straighteners and disinfectants.

saccharin: Artificial sweetener more than three hundred times sweeter than table sugar. Once added to canned vegetables to mask sour taste. Later used by consumers as a sugar substitute. In the early 1970s, researchers claimed that saccharin caused bladder cancer in rats. After 1977, FDA required warning labels on foods and beverages containing saccharin. By 2000, new research had shown that rat digestion differed from human. Because saccharin's effect did not apply to humans, the warning label was dropped. Today, **ALLOWED** in foods and beverages with label listing it as an ingredient.

salicylic acid: Kills bacteria. Once added as a preservative to canned fruits and pickles. If ingested, causes headaches, dizziness, nausea, and vomiting. Overexposure to it is thought to cause genetic defects and damage to the nervous system and kidneys. **NOT ALLOWED IN FOODS.** Today, used in dandruff shampoo, wart remover, and acne treatment.

saltpeter (potassium nitrate/sodium nitrate): Preservative used to cure meat, poultry, and fish. Prevents growth of bacteria and holds meat's color. Today, sodium nitrate often replaces potassium nitrate as a food preservative. **ALLOWED** in deli meat, hotdogs, ham, bacon, and smoked fish. Saltpeter is also an ingredient in fireworks and fertilizer.

sulfites/sulfurous acid: Stop microbe growth. Used to prepare dried fruits and wine and added as a preservative to stop fruits and vegetables from turning brown. Today, **ALLOWED** in certain foods. Because some people are allergic to sulfites, products containing them must be labeled. They are **NOT ALLOWED** on raw fruits and vegetables.

GLOSSARY

abolitionist: a person who wanted to end slavery.

adulteration: a change to a food or beverage that produces an inferior product, which deceives or harms the consumer.

anatomy: the study of the body's parts.

anemia: weakness, exhaustion, and pale skin caused by reduced numbers of blood cells.

arsenic: a chemical once widely used in medicines. Ingestion in low amounts affects digestion. In high amounts, it can cause liver damage and death. May cause cancer. Not allowed as a food additive today.

bacteria: microscopic one-celled organisms.

boarding house: a place where people pay for a room and meals. The Poison Squad volunteers received all meals (board) at the Bureau of Chemistry, but they did not live there.

coal-tar colors: dyes originally made from coal, and today from petroleum. Many are thought to cause cancer and are strictly regulated by the FDA.

cocaine: an addictive drug made from leaves of the coca plant. Today, legally available only as a prescription drug used by doctors to numb pain during certain medical procedures.

codeine: a narcotic derived from opium; used as a painkiller and cough medicine.

colic: frequent crying in infants due to physical discomfort such as abdominal pain.

diethylene glycol: the deadly ingredient in Elixir Sulfanilamide.

elixir: a sweet liquid medicine containing alcohol.

glucose: a sugary syrup inexpensively made by combining cornstarch, water, and an acid; used as a substitute for honey, maple syrup, and cane sugar.

heroin: a highly addictive narcotic drug derived from morphine.

lead: a chemical that can accumulate in the body and affect all organs. It is especially harmful to the nervous system and to brain development in children.

mercury: a toxic element that damages kidneys, brain, and nervous system. May also affect heart, lungs, and digestive system. FDA limits the mercury content allowed in fish.

microbe: a microscopic organism, such as a bacterium or virus.

misbranding: selling a product with a false or misleading label or packaging.

morphine: an addictive narcotic derived from opium; legally available only with a doctor's prescription.

muckraker: a journalist who raises public awareness about corruption and social ills, such as hazardous working conditions and unsafe foods and drugs. President Theodore Roosevelt coined the term in a 1906 speech.

narcotic: an addictive drug that induces sleep and dulls pain. Examples: opium, morphine, codeine, heroin.

nostrum: a quack medicine.

opium: an addictive narcotic drug made from the opium poppy that relieves pain and produces sleep.

over-the-counter drugs: medicines that do not require a doctor's prescription.

para-phenylenediamine: the chemical in Lash Lure that caused blindness. Today, it's approved for use in hair dye with a required warning label about allergic reactions and dangers of applying around the eyes.

pathology: the study of diseases.

pesticide: a substance used to kill insects and weeds.

pharmacology: the study of drugs, their uses, and their effect on the body.

physiology: the study of how the body works.

poison: a substance that causes extreme harm or death, even when taken in small amounts.

preservative: a substance added to food to prevent spoiling and decay.

Progressives: activists during the 1890s to 1920s who called for reforms in politics, society, and the economy.

proprietary medicines: tonics, tablets, and other nostrums advertised to cure or treat various illnesses; usually ineffective. The manufacturer kept the ingredients secret. Also called **patent**

medicines, although these drugs were rarely registered at the U.S. Patent Office.

radium: an element that gives off radiation, damaging body cells. Can cause cancer and other illnesses. No longer permitted in food or cosmetics.

smallpox: a contagious, often fatal disease caused by a virus. Symptoms include high fever and skin sores.

socialist: a person who advocates an economic system without private business ownership in which all members of society share work and profits.

sulfanilamide: a drug used to treat infections by killing bacteria, today available by prescription.

thalidomide: a drug used as a sleeping aid and to ease nausea in pregnant women. Caused damage to developing babies.

thallium: highly toxic chemical once used to remove hair (the ingredient in Koremlu) and to kill rats and mice. Caused blindness and nervous system problems. No longer allowed in food or cosmetics.

tonic: a medicine advertised to increase strength and energy.

toxic: causing extreme harm or death.

tuberculosis: a serious and sometimes fatal lung disease caused by a bacterium.

TIMELINE

1844
Harvey Wiley
born in Indiana.

1861–65
American Civil War.

1883
Wiley hired as chief
of the Division of
Chemistry.

1896
William McKinley
elected president.

1897
James Wilson
becomes secretary
of agriculture.

1898
Spanish-
American War.

1901
Division of
Chemistry renamed
Bureau of Chemistry.

President McKinley
assassinated;
Theodore Roosevelt
becomes president.

1902–03
Wiley conducts the first
Poison Squad experiment.

1906
FEBRUARY—
The Jungle is
published.

JUNE 30—
President Theodore
Roosevelt signs
Food and Drugs
Act and Meat
Inspection
Amendment.

1905
DECEMBER—
President Theodore
Roosevelt mentions
need for pure food
and drugs law in his
message to Congress.

1905–06
Collier's publishes
proprietary medicine
exposés.

1903–06
*Ladies' Home
Journal* publishes
proprietary
medicine exposés.

1909
William Howard Taft becomes president.

1911
Wiley marries Anna Campbell Kelton.

Coca-Cola trial.

1912
Wiley resigns from Bureau of Chemistry; becomes an editor at *Good Housekeeping* magazine.

Woodrow Wilson elected president.

1914–18
World War I.

1930
JUNE 30—
Harvey Wiley dies in Washington, DC.

Former Bureau of Chemistry now officially called the Food and Drug Administration (FDA).

1932
Franklin Roosevelt elected president.

1933
FDA displays the Chamber of Horrors.

100,000,000 Guinea Pigs is published.

1937
Elixir Sulfanilamide kills 107 Americans.

1936
American Chamber of Horrors is published.

2018
FDA employs more than seventeen thousand people.

1988
FDA becomes part of the Department of Health and Human Services.

1962
Kefauver-Harris Drug Amendments passed.

1961
Reports from the medical community connect thalidomide to birth defects.

1938
President Franklin Roosevelt signs Food, Drug, and Cosmetic Act.

Advertisement for a quack medical device
claiming to cure headaches and insomnia
with magnets, from the late 1800s

MORE TO EXPLORE*

THE FOOD AND DRUG ADMINISTRATION (FDA)

U.S. Food & Drug Administration.
fda.gov
  Explore the agency's website to learn more about its history and current work and see the latest recalls and alerts.

"Defect Levels Handbook."
U.S. Food & Drug Administration.
fda.gov/food/guidanceregulation/ guidancedocumentsregulatory information/ucm056174.htm
  Check out—if you dare—the FDA's acceptable limits for insect parts and rodent hair in foods.

"How Does the FDA Approve New Drugs?"
YouTube.
youtube.com/watch?v=UbRc4_ alpmw
  Learn the steps required before a new drug can be sold in the U.S., posted by Testtube News.

USFoodandDrugAdmin.
YouTube.
youtube.com/user/ USFoodandDrugAdmin
  At the FDA's YouTube channel, you can find videos on a range of topics such as Lyme disease treatment, head lice prevention, sunscreen basics, and antimicrobial resistance. The FDA's History Vault videos include interesting stories from the agency's history. Check these out:

■ "Welcome to FDA's White Oak Campus."
youtube.com/ watch?v=DqimZYtaqHw
  Get an overview of the FDA's work today at its Maryland center.

■ "The American Chamber of Horrors."
youtube.com/watch?v=Zu_ erFKxHj8
  Learn how a 1930s FDA exhibit led to passage of the 1938 Food, Drug, and Cosmetic Act.

■ "From the FDA Vault: A Calculating History."
youtube.com/watch?v=XiNA_ aMaH_o
  Find out about the Thacher Calculating Instrument used by Wiley's Bureau of Chemistry for complicated calculations.

Websites active at time of publication

131

Three of the Orgone Accumulators, 1950s quack medical devices advertised to use a mysterious force to cure diseases

■ "From the FDA Vault: A Shocking ExerciZe." **youtube.com/watch?v=ct7bqOVURg8**
These quack devices were advertised to treat medical conditions, but they were useless and sometimes dangerous.

■ "From the FDA Vault: Trying Times." **youtube.com/watch?v=ieFQsdhJgdg**
See how FDA inspectors sampled and tested products.

■ "From the FDA Vault: Radiating Shoe Sales." **youtube.com/watch?v=cfALJUSmzzk**
This shoe-fitting device exposed salesclerks and customers, especially children, to dangerous radiation.

FOOD AND ITS SAFETY

"Kids World—Food Safety." North Carolina Department of Agriculture and Consumer Services, Raleigh, NC. **ncagr.gov/cyber/kidswrld/foodsafe/index.htm**
Explore nutrition and food labels, and learn about microbes that make food dangerous.

RADIUM

"The Radium Girls."
SciShow on YouTube.
**youtube.com/
watch?v=galqlW6VcMY**

"Glowing in the Dark—The Radium
Girls."
Today I Found Out on YouTube.
**youtube.com/
watch?v=7875DVDdmnE**
Watch two videos summarizing
the story of the radium craze,
glow-in-the-dark watches, and the
dial painters whose illnesses awoke
the medical community and
government authorities to the
dangers of radium.

THALIDOMIDE

"The Shadow of the Thalidomide
Tragedy | Retro Report | The *New
York Times*."
YouTube.
**youtube.com/
watch?v=41n3mDoVbvk**
This 2013 video summarizes the
thalidomide case, including
interviews with victims and Dr.
Frances Kelsey. Learn how the drug
is used today.

"President Kennedy speaks of a
new bill to deal strictly with
hazardous drugs available in the
market."
Critical Past.
**criticalpast.com/
video/65675042811_President-
Kennedy_delivering-a-speech_
food-and-drugs-administration_
hazardous-drugs**
Watch a 1962 video of President
John Kennedy speaking about the
thalidomide tragedy and the need
for stronger laws to help the FDA
safeguard the public from
dangerous drugs.

POISON CHEMICALS

*Poison: Deadly Deeds, Perilous
Professions, and Murderous
Medicines* by Sarah Albee. New
York: Crown Books for Young
Readers, 2017.
This nonfiction book for young
readers describes how ingested
chemicals have injured and killed
humans throughout history—
intentionally (as a murder weapon)
and accidentally.

AUTHOR'S NOTE

The Poison Squads were more than several dozen young men brave enough to "eat the fare." Wiley's Hygienic Tables are only part of an intriguing story with a cast of passionate, determined, and sometimes flawed characters.

I begin each book project uncertain where my research will take me. The story of the Poison Eaters turned out to be bigger than I expected. As I learned, so is the story of the Food and Drug Administration.

Today, the FDA's actions affect much of our lives: Every meal we eat at home or in a restaurant. Every trip to the doctor, dentist, or hospital. The care we give our pets. The creams we put on our skin, and the shampoo we use to wash our hair.

Most of us don't think twice about the safety of each bite of food or dose of medicine. For that, we can thank the FDA, which started from a few diligent chemists in a basement laboratory.

Harvey Wiley, the Father of the FDA, is central to this story. I kicked off my research by reading Wiley's own words in his autobiography, scientific publications, congressional testimonies, and *Good Housekeeping* articles. Exploring his papers at the Library of Congress, I discovered diaries and private letters that broadened my view of him. To find out what others said about Wiley (both positive and negative), I located letters and autobiographies by his family, friends, and professional associates. Newspaper editorials, magazine articles, and politicians' speeches provided additional insight into Wiley and his pure-food quest.

To understand what food and drugs were like in the 1800s and early 1900s, I read the Bureau of Chemistry reports, scientific and medical journals, the muckrakers' work, newspaper accounts of the pure-food movement, and advertising from the period. Books and articles by historians filled in details about food manufacturing, proprietary medicines, and the 1906 bill's twenty-five-year journey through Congress. Information from the

FDA History Office was particularly helpful.

Following the story into the present, I relied on current FDA publications, chemistry and food science experts, and recent books and articles about the safety of food and medicine.

Photographs brought the scenes and actors to life for me, and I have shared many of the images with readers.

Every day, I see and hear advertising claims as outrageous as those of the quack medicine companies one hundred years ago: A foolproof way to have clear, radiant skin. The revolutionary method to freeze off body fat at home, for only $100. Countless products promise to improve your appearance, boost your strength, and soothe aches and pains. Just like a century ago, people buy them.

While government oversight has increased, it doesn't completely protect us from fraud and danger. Should we expect that? How many restrictions should there be on what we buy and sell? Do the officials who impose restrictions always make the correct decision? Should we have more freedom to choose the products we use, even if it means making mistakes?

These questions are as controversial today as they were in Harvey Wiley's time. The debate continues.
—G.J.

Harvey Wiley's Civil War diary and a page from his August 15, 1864, entry.

SOURCE NOTES

The source of each quotation in this book is found below. The citation indicates the first words of the quotation and its document source. The sources are listed either in the bibliography or below.

The following abbreviations are used:

AUTO—*Harvey W. Wiley: An Autobiography*

WP—Wiley Papers, Library of Congress

CHAPTER ONE
EMBALMED BEES *and* OTHER DELICACIES (Page 8)

"There is Death . . .": Accum, vii.

"this preparation . . .": Advertisement for Cocaine Toothache Drops, 1885, from National Library of Medicine.

CHAPTER TWO
FARM BOY (Page 13)

"I found myself . . .": AUTO, 138.

"because of my parental . . .": AUTO, 58.

"Father, I am going . . .": AUTO, 60.

"Very well . . .": Preston Wiley, quoted in same as above.

"Prepared 'to do . . .": Wiley diary, September 7, 1863, WP, Box 213.

"their polluted . . .": Wiley diary, June 18, 1864, WP, Box 213.

"with a faith . . .": Wiley diary, June 7, 1864, WP, Box 213.

"This and that . . ." and "without much . . .": AUTO, p. 101.

"My aversion . . ." and "that I felt . . .": AUTO, p. 117.

"to believe that tremendous . . .": AUTO, p. 154.

CHAPTER THREE
CHEMICAL FEAST (Page 21)

"Poisonous adulterations . . .": Wedderburn, p. 10.

"We have been greatly . . .": Trustee Dobblebower, quoted by Wiley in AUTO, p. 157.

"We are deeply . . .": same as above.

"But the most grave . . ." and "Professor Wiley . . .": same as above, p. 158.

"Gentlemen, I am . . ." and "I desire . . .": Wiley, AUTO, p. 158.

"highly poisonous . . .": Wiley, *Foods and Their Adulteration*, p. 194.

"The practice . . ." and "is reprehensible.": Wiley, same as above, p. 371.

"The poor man" and "while entitled . . .": same as above, pp. 383–84.

"Be sure you are . . .": Preston Wiley, quoted in AUTO, p. 236.

"the consumer will get . . .": Wiley, quoted in "The Man Who Is Leading the Fight for Pure Food," *Washington Times*, November 20, 1904.

"terror of . . .": AUTO, p. 38.

"I never write . . ." and "since I depend . . .": letter from Wiley to J. F. Mitchell, City Editor of *Scranton* [PA] *Truth*, December 7, 1903, WP, Box 8.

"RUDE AWAKENING": Alice Lakey, in *Federation Bulletin*, November 1906, p. 87, quoted in Goodwin, p. 48.

"the sweepings of . . ." and "Much of our grape . . ." and "used 1,000 pounds . . .": Alice Lakey, quoted in "The Terrors that Lurk in Adulterated Foods," *New York Times*, December 13, 1905.

"A rude awakening" and "convinced . . .": Alice Lakey, in *Federation Bulletin*, November 1906, p. 87, quoted in Goodwin, p. 48.

CHAPTER FOUR
The POISON EATERS (Page 36)

Headline from the *Kalispell* [MT] *Bee*, May 5, 1903

"We told them that they . . .": Wiley, *The History of a Crime*, p. 67.

"I arrive at . . .": AUTO, p. 215.

"would naturally follow . . .": AUTO, p. 216.

"ordinary preservatives . . .": Wiley, *The History of a Crime*, p. 66.

"We told them, of course . . .": same as above, p. 67.

"whether they wanted . . .": same as above.

"Second Day . . .": "Eating by Rigid Rule," *Washington Post*, December 22, 1902.

"Gloomy Christmas Dinner": "Borax Begins to Tell," *Washington Post*, December 26, 1902.

"'poison eaters'": "Testing Adulterated Foods," *Wichita Daily Eagle*, December 12, 1902.

"'poison' capsules": "Poison Eaters Fail to Come to Weight," *Washington Times*, December 18, 1902.

"poison squad": "Ceylon and India Tea," advertisement, *New-York Tribune*, December 8, 1902.

"Our young man . . ." and "no doubt . . .": letter from Scott Bone to Wiley, December 24, 1902, WP, Box 48.

"the most widely . . .": Wiley, *The History of a Crime*, p. 67.

"Old Borax": "Testing Food Stuffs at Appraiser's Store," *New York Times*, September 18, 1904.

"If ever you should . . .": Song by Lew Dockstader, week of October 4, 1903, quoted in Wiley, *The History of a Crime*, p. 77.

"Throbbing pains . . .": Volunteer #2 Daily Chart, Bureau of Chemistry, February 8, 1905, FDA History Office.

"disturbance to . . .": Wiley, quoted in "Danger in Food Preservatives," *Washington Post*, November 16, 1904.

"There can never be any agreement . . .": Wiley, *Foods and Adulteration*, p. 40.

"where it can possibly . . .": Wiley, "Methods of Studying . . .," *Journal of the Franklin Institute*, March 1904, p. 178.

"I say . . ." and "that the men . . .": Wiley, quoted by James Harvey Young in "The Science and Morals of Metabolism: Catsup and Benzoate of Soda," *Journal of the History of Medicine and Allied Sciences*, January 1968, p. 90.

"poisonous adulterants": "Poison Squad Blamed," *Evening Star* [Washington, DC], November 21, 1906.

"that the government . . .": "Wants Wilson to Tell about Poison Squad," *Washington Times*, December 22, 1906.

"it is a bad practice . . .": same as above.

"great mathematical . . .": Wiley, "Methods of Studying the Effect of Preservatives," p. 171.

"Dr. Wiley is doing . . .": Dr. Edward Gudeman, quoted in "Poison Squad Man Attacked," *New York Sun*, April 2, 1905.

"You could take any . . ." and "give them . . .": Professor William Hoff, quoted in "Poison Squad Man Attacked," same as above.

"I've been roasted . . ." and "I'm perfectly . . .": Wiley, quoted in "Poison Squad Man Attacked," *New York Sun*, April 2, 1905.

"If any American . . .": same as above.

"Poor mothers doped . . .": AUTO, p. 207.

"these glaring evils": AUTO, p. 200.

"should know the exact . . .": Wiley, *Foods and Adulteration*, p. 186.

CHAPTER FIVE
MORPHINE, MEAT, *and* MUCKRAKERS (Page 54)

"The eyes of the people . . .": Edward Bok, "A Few Words to the W.C.T.U.," *Ladies' Home Journal*, September 1904, p. 16.

"I fear that this man . . .": AUTO, p. 221.

"I consider it . . ." and "and one which . . .": AUTO, p. 223.

"I will let you off . . .": Roosevelt, quoted by Wiley, AUTO, p. 223.

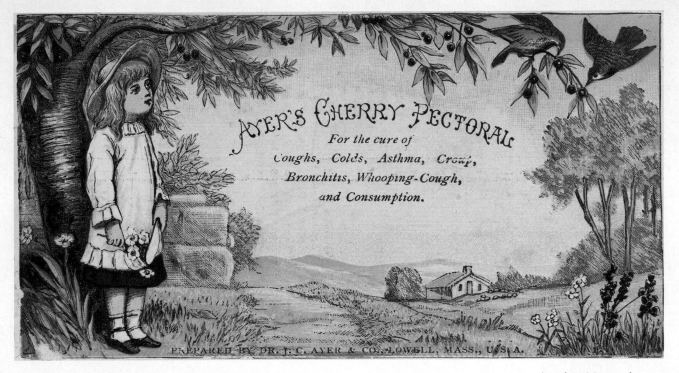

An advertising card from the 1880s

"If the baby . . .": Maud Banfield, "The Journal's Trained Nurse, About Patent
    Medicines," *Ladies' Home Journal*, May 1903, p. 26.
"Sooner or later . . .": Edward Bok, "The 'Patent-Medicine' Curse," *Ladies' Home
    Journal*, May 1904, p. 18.
"She has a right . . .": Edward Bok, "To You: A Personal Word," *Ladies' Home Journal*,
    February 1906, p. 20.
"relieve[s] depression . . .": Adams, *Great American Fraud*, p. 17.
"Even small doses . . ." and "cause that craving . . .": same as above, p. 15.
"lay like . . .": Nora, quoted in Adams, *Great American Fraud*, p. 40.
"a law to regulate . . .": Roosevelt, quoted in "President's Message to Congress,"
    Washington Post, December 6, 1905.
"I am frightened . . .": A. C. Fraser, quoted in AUTO, p. 213.
"I have never . . ." and "and perhaps . . .": AUTO, p. 213.
"Is there a man . . . who would put . . .": AUTO, p. 214.
"Is there a man . . . who would so adulterate . . .": same as above.
"give one man . . .": Walter Williams, quoted in *The History of a Crime*, p. 3.
"Are we going to take . . .": Nelson Aldrich, quoted in Sullivan, p. 532.
"It is the purpose . . .": Porter McCumber, quoted in same as above.
"To the Workingmen . . .": Sinclair, *The Jungle*, dedication.
"floor was half an inch . . .": Sinclair, *The Jungle*, p. 45.
"where the workers . . .": same as above, p. 161.
"fell into the vats . . .": same as above, p. 117.

"Mary had a little . . .": *New York Evening Post*, quoted in Sullivan, p. 541.

"I aimed at . . .": Upton Sinclair, "What Life Means to Me," *Cosmopolitan*, October 1906.

"Is this no longer . . ." and "but by the . . .": Alice Lakey, "Pure Food of All Kinds,"
    New York Times, June 13, 1906.

"The people are demanding . . .": William H. Ryan, *Congressional Record*, 59 Congress
    Session 1, June 22, 1906, p. 8988.

"A Pure Food Law at Last": *Los Angeles Times*, June 30, 1906.

"Pure-Food Bill Wins": *Washington Post*, June 24, 1906.

"the greatest . . .": Wiley, *The History of a Crime*, p. 52.

"Relentless Foe . . .": "The Man Who Is Leading the Fight for Pure Food," *Washington
    Times*, November 20, 1904.

"How does a general . . .": AUTO, p. 231.

CHAPTER SIX
"JANITOR *of the* PEOPLE'S INSIDES" (Page 70)

"Janitor of the . . .": "Poison Squad to Try Soda," *New York Sun*, November 24, 1907.

"No honest man . . .": Wiley, quoted in "Wiley Warns Advertisers," *New York Sun*,
    November 11, 1908.

"When in doubt . . .": Wiley, *1001 Tests of Foods*, p. xiii.

"He had the greatest . . ." and "to take the wrong . . .": AUTO, pp. 190–91.

"Do you think . . .": Roosevelt, quoted by Wiley in "T.R.'s 'Poor Food' Record,"
    New York Times, October 3, 1912.

"I do not think . . ." and "I have tried . . .": Wiley, quoted in same as above.

"Gentlemen, if this . . .": Roosevelt, quoted by Wiley in same as above.

"My firm saved . . .": James S. Sherman, quoted by Wiley in same as above.

"Yes, Mr. President" and "and every one . . .": Wiley, in same as above.

"Anybody who says . . .": Roosevelt, quoted by Wiley in same as above.

"tests and investigations . . ." and "tests when made . . .": "No Appropriations for the
    Poison Squad," *New York Sun*, April 3, 1908.

"was the basis . . .": Wiley, *The History of a Crime*, 163.

"The trouble with . . .": letter from Roosevelt to Henry Hurd Rusby, January 7, 1909,
    in Roosevelt, p. 1467.

"I expect to give . . .": letter from Taft to Ward, March 24, 1919, quoted in Pringle, p. 729.

"It was not a difficult . . ." and "but it was . . .": AUTO, p. 2.

"a cowardly . . ." and "YOU ARE RIGHT. THE FUTURE . . ." and "You are the ONE
    MAN . . .": letter from Alice Lakey to Harvey W. Wiley, July 6, 1911, WP, Box 91.

"LIQUID BREEZE": Coca-Cola advertisement, *The Independent*, June 30, 1910.

"I consider caffeine . . ." and "It creates a desire . . .": Dr. John Musser, quoted in
    "Caffeine's Effects Bad, Say Experts," *Atlanta Georgian*, March 17, 1911.

"It will not be long . . ." and "and soon we . . .": letter from Wiley to Norman Hapgood,
    March 31, 1911, quoted in Coppin, p. 151.

"I saw the fundamental . . .": AUTO, p. 289.

"left to come . . .": Wiley resignation letter, quoted in "Dr. Wiley Resigns; Friction the Cause," *New York Daily Tribune*, March 16, 1912.

"I was in the midst . . .": AUTO, pp. 165–66.

"I know that you . . .": letter from Harriet Taylor Upton to Annie C. Kelton, January 17, 1911, WP, Box 88.

"Mr. President . . .": quoted by Anna Wiley in "Statement about Mrs. Harvey W. Wiley by herself, July 16, 1947," Anna Wiley Papers, Box 76.

CHAPTER SEVEN
OLD BORAX (Page 86)

"Science fails . . .": Wiley, "Applications of Chemistry to Public Welfare," p. 54.

"Women Weep . . .": *Buffalo* [NY] *Courier*, March 16, 1912.

"The Department is . . .": *Collier's Weekly*, quoted in "Effects of Dr. Wiley's Exit," *Literary Digest*, March 30, 1912, p. 626.

"He was the cause . . .": *Salt Lake Herald-Republican*, quoted in same as above.

"most serious . . .": letter from Alice Lakey to Taft, May 21, 1912, quoted in Pringle, p. 730.

"very earnest . . ." and "a constant . . .": draft of letter from Taft to G. P. McQuade, January 24, 1913, quoted in Pringle, p. 731.

"I am naturally not . . .": Wiley, quoted in "T.R.'s 'Poor Food' Record," *New York Times*, October 3, 1912.

"By their fruits . . .": same as above.

"In this favorable . . ." and "I have had . . .": Wiley, *1001 Tests*, p. xx.

"free from injurious . . .": AUTO, p. 304.

"The drugs . . .": Wiley, "An Opium Bonfire," *Good Housekeeping*, August 1912.

"Few of them are . . ." and "but they are all . . .": Wiley, "Dr. Wiley's Department," *Good Housekeeping*, July 1913.

"One dollar . . .": same as above.

"Almost all Americans . . ." and "We are extremists . . .": Wiley, quoted in Edward Marshall, "He Believes Americans Over-Eat, Over-Drink and Over-Everything and Thereby Slowly Kill Themselves," *New York Times*, March 19, 1911.

"Work never killed . . ." and "Rusting out . . .": Wiley, quoted in Elna Harwood Wharton, "Dr. Wiley's Recipe for Longevity," *Forecast Magazine*, ca. 1926, WP, Box 211.

"If the Bureau . . ." Wiley, *The History of a Crime*, p. 401.

"our foods . . .": same as above, p. 402.

"If I had . . ." and "I would choose . . .": AUTO, p. 13.

"As a result . . ." and "the span of . . .": "Dr. Harvey W. Wiley," *Washington Post*, July 1, 1930.

"He served . . .": W. D. Bigelow, "Wiley—The Public Servant," *In Memoriam Harvey Washington Wiley*, Association of Official Agricultural Chemists, 1930, WP, Box 211.

CHAPTER EIGHT
RADIOACTIVE MIRACLES (Page 93)

"Thousands of people . . .": "Radium Bath Sale," advertisement in *Washington Star*, October 19, 1923.

"He will take rank . . ." and "among the greatest . . .": Sinclair, "The House of Wonder," *Pearson's Magazine*, June 1922.

"If you are sick" and "don't get . . .": Advertisement, *Seattle Star*, October 18, 1922.

"strongly radioactive": Alexander O. Gettler and Charles Norris, "Poisoning from Drinking Radium Water," *Journal of the American Medical Association*, February 11, 1933.

"Eben M. Byers . . .": "Eben M. Byers Dies of Radium Poisoning," *New York Times*, April 1, 1932.

"Is the Federal . . .": "Hands tied," *New York World-Telegram*, April 9, 1932, quoted in Lamb, p. 74.

"detrimental to health . . .": Gettler and Norris, same as above.

"Radiates Personality": Lash Lure advertisement, from FDA Chamber of Horrors display.

"I started losing . . .": letter from anonymous woman to Roosevelt, ca. 1933, quoted in Lamb, p. 33.

"it is exceedingly . . .": Kallet and Schlink, p. 10.

"several decades": same as above.

"The moment it enters . . .": Listerine advertisement, December 1933, unidentified magazine, Flickr, "Listerine-Lasting Antiseptic!"

"If this muck-raking . . ." and "it will not . . .": letter from Campbell to Simon Sobeloff, 1933, quoted in Young, *The Medical Messiahs*, p. 157.

CHAPTER NINE
RASPBERRY COUGH SYRUP (Page 105)

"It is time . . .": Franklin Roosevelt, "The President's Message to Congress," March 22, 1935, quoted in Lamb, p. 333.

"I have just . . ." and "It is high . . ." and "It should have . . .": Eleanor Roosevelt, quoted in Genevieve Forbes Herrick, "Mrs. Roosevelt Talks of Truth in Advertising," *Chicago Daily Tribune*, October 24, 1933.

"The great majority . . ." and "Present legislation . . .": Franklin Roosevelt, "The President's Message to Congress," March 22, 1935, quoted in Lamb, p. 334.

"My mother has been . . .": letter from "Hazel Fay Brown" to Mr. President [Franklin Roosevelt], no date, quoted in Lamb, p. 327.

"Hay; fragments of . . .": Lamb, p. 253.

"We can see her . . .": letter from Marie Nidiffer to Roosevelt, quoted by Carol Ballentine in "Taste of Raspberries, Taste of Death: The 1937 Elixir Sulfanilamide Incident," *FDA Consumer Magazine*, June 1981.

"Death Drug": "'Death Drug' Hunt Covered 15 States," *New York Times*, November 26, 1937.

"Deadly 'Elixir'": Gerald G. Gross, "Seizure of Deadly 'Elixir' Saves Marylander as U.S. Hastens to Check Toll Already at 29," *Washington Post*, October 23, 1937.

"It makes a tremendous . . ." and "It will not only . . .": Helen Hall, quoted in Anne Petersen, "Women Eager to Note Effect of Food Laws," *New York Times*, May 7, 1939.

CHAPTER TEN
The WATCHDOGS (Page 114)

"In next to no time . . .": Kelsey, p. 75.

"non-toxic" and "completely harmless . . .": Chemie Grunenthal company, quoted in Hilts, p. 149.

"TOO GLOWING": Kelsey, p. 52.

"very unimpressed": Kelsey, quoted in Morton Mintz, "'Heroine' of FDA Keeps Bad Drug Off of Market," *Washington Post*, July 15, 1962.

"The claims . . .": Kelsey, p. 52.

"This was really . . .": Kelsey, p. 78.

"100% Natural" and "No Side Effects": Label of Hyland's Baby Teething Tablets, fda.gov/ForConsumers/ConsumerUpdates/ucm230762.htm, Retrieved February 2, 2018.

"have been safely . . .": Iris R. Bell, Director of Scientific Affairs, hylands.com/products/hylands-baby-teething-tablets, Retrieved December 31, 2017.

"toward improving . . .": Wiley, *The History of a Crime*, p. x.

"Certainly it is . . ." and "in that long . . .": AUTO, p. 232.

AUTHOR'S NOTE (Page 134)

"eat the fare": photograph, U.S. Food and Drug Administration, History Office.

BIBLIOGRAPHY

*Indicates a primary source

*Accum, Fredrick. *Treatise on Adulterations of Food, and Culinary Poisons.* 2nd ed. London: Longman, Hurst, Rees, Orme, and Brown, 1820.

Adams, Samuel Hopkins. *The Great American Fraud: A Series of Articles on the Patent Medicine Evil*, Reprinted from *Collier's Weekly.* Chicago: Press of the American Medical Association, 1906.

Anderson, Oscar E., Jr. *The Health of a Nation: Harvey W. Wiley and the Fight for Pure Food.* Chicago: University of Chicago Press, 1958.

Bjorkman, Edwin. "Our Debt to Dr. Wiley, A Public Servant Who Is a Hard Fighter for Pure Food and Is Generally on the Winning Side." *The World's Work*, January 1910: 12443–48.

Blum, Deborah. *The Poisoner's Handbook: Murder and the Birth of Forensic Medicine in Jazz Age New York.* New York: Penguin, 2010.

Carson, Gerald H. "Who Put the Borax in Dr. Wiley's Butter?" *American Heritage*, August 1956.

Civitello, Linda. *Baking Powder Wars: The Cutthroat Food Fight That Revolutionized Cooking.* Urbana: University of Illinois Press, 2017.

Coppin, Clayton A., and Jack High. *The Politics of Purity: Harvey Washington Wiley and the Origins of Federal Food Policy.* Ann Arbor: University of Michigan Press, 1999.

Courtwright, David T. *Dark Paradise: A History of Opiate Addiction in America.* Cambridge, MA: Harvard University Press, 2001.

Davis, O. K. "The Case of Dr. Wiley." *Hampton Columbian Magazine*, October 1911: 469–81.

Duncan, Charles M. *Eat, Drink, and Be Wary.* Lanham, MD: Rowman & Littlefield, 2015.

Evershed, Richard, and Nicola Temple. *Sorting the Beef from the Bull: The Science of Food Fraud Forensics.* London: Bloomsbury, 2016.

FDA Consumer Magazine, the Centennial Edition, January–February 2006.

Finck, Henry Theophilus. *Food and Flavor: A Gastronomic Guide to Health and Good Living*. New York: The Century Co., 1913.

Frank, Patricia, and M. Alice Ottoboni. *The Dose Makes the Poison: A Plain-Language Guide to Toxicology*. 3rd ed. Hoboken, NJ: John Wiley & Sons, 2011.

Goodwin, Lorine Swainston. *The Pure Food, Drink, and Drug Crusaders, 1879–1914*. Jefferson, NC: McFarland, 1999.

Hamowy, Ronald. "Medical Disasters and the Growth of the FDA." *Independent Policy Reports*. Oakland, CA: The Independent Institute, 2010.

Hilts, Philip J. *Protecting America's Health: The FDA, Business, and One Hundred Years of Regulation*. Chapel Hill, NC: University of North Carolina Press, 2003.

Janssen, Wallace F. "Inside the Poison Squad: How Food Additive Regulation Began." *Association of Food and Drug Officials Quarterly Bulletin*, April 1987: 68–72.

Junod, Suzanne W. "Harvey Wiley's 'Poison Squad': Food Additive Safety." [PowerPoint slides]. October 21, 2012. FDA History Office, U.S. Food and Drug Administration.

Junod, Suzanne White. "Food Standards in the United States: The Case of the Peanut Butter and Jelly Sandwich." In *Food, Science, Policy and Regulation in the Twentieth Century: International and Comparative Perspectives*, edited by David F. Smith and Jim Phillips. New York: Routledge, 2000.

Kallet, Arthur, and F. J. Schlink. *100,000,000 Guinea Pigs: Dangers in Everyday Foods, Drugs, and Cosmetics*. New York: Vanguard Press, 1933.

*Kelsey, Frances Oldham. *Autobiographical Reflections*. Oral History Program. FDA History Office, U.S. Food and Drug Administration. fda.gov/downloads/AboutFDA/ WhatWeDo/History/OralHistories/SelectedOralHistoryTranscripts/UCM406132.pdf. Accessed February 8, 2018.

Lamb, Ruth deForest. *American Chamber of Horrors: The Truth about Food and Drugs*. New York: Farrar & Rinehart, 1936.

Levenstein, Harvey. *Fear of Food: A History of Why We Worry about What We Eat*. Chicago: University of Chicago Press, 2012.

Lewis, Carol. "The 'Poison Squad' and the Advent of Food and Drug Regulation." *FDA Consumer Magazine*, November–December 2002.

Macklis, Roger M. "The Great Radium Scandal." *Scientific American*, August 1993: 94–99.

Mullan, Fitzhugh. *Plagues and Politics: The Story of the United States Public Health Service*. New York: Basic Books, 1989.

Pendergrast, Mark. *For God, Country & Coca-Cola: The Definitive History of the Great American Soft Drink and the Company that Makes It.* 2nd ed. New York: Basic Books, 2000.

Piott, Steven L. *American Reformers, 1870–1920: Progressives in Word and Deed.* Lanham, MD: Rowman & Littlefield, 2006.

Pringle, Henry F. *The Life and Times of William Howard Taft: A Biography, Volume 2.* New York: Farrar & Rinehart, 1939.

Ravenel, Mazyck P., ed. *A Half Century of Public Health.* New York: American Public Health Association, 1921.

*Roosevelt, Theodore. *The Letters of Theodore Roosevelt, Volume 6.* Elting E. Morison, ed. Cambridge, MA: Harvard University Press, 1952.

Ryan, John M. *Food Fraud.* London: Academic Press/Elsevier, 2016.

*Sinclair, Upton. *The Autobiography of Upton Sinclair.* New York: Harcourt, Brace & World, 1962.

*_____. *The Jungle.* New York: Doubleday, Page & Company, 1906.

Sullivan, Mark. *Our Times, The United States 1900-1925: Volume 2, America Finding Herself.* New York: Charles Scribner's Sons, 1927.

Swann, John P. "How Chemists Pushed for Chemical Protection—The Food and Drugs Act of 1906." *Chemical Heritage*, Summer 2006: 6–11.

*U.S. Department of Agriculture, Bureau of Chemistry. *Foods and Food Adulterants.* Bulletin No. 13. Washington, DC: Government Printing Office, 1887–1902.

*_____. *Influence of Food Preservatives and Artificial Colors on Digestion and Health.* Bulletin No. 84, parts 1–5. Washington, DC: Government Printing Office, 1904–08.

"U.S. Food and Drug Administration." *U.S. Department of Health and Human Services.* fda.gov.

Wax, Paul M. "Elixirs, Diluents, and the Passage of the 1938 Federal Food, Drug and Cosmetic Act." *Annals of Internal Medicine*, March 15, 1995: 456–61.

Wedderburn, Alex. J. *A Popular Treatise on the Extent and Character of Food Adulterations.* Bulletin No. 25. U.S. Department of Agriculture, Division of Chemistry. Washington, DC: Government Printing Office, 1890.

Whorton, James. *Before Silent Spring: Pesticides and Public Health in Pre-DDT America.* Princeton, NJ: Princeton University Press, 1974.

*Wiley, Anna Kelton. Papers. Manuscript Division, Library of Congress, Washington, DC.

*Wiley, H. W. "The Adulteration of Food." *Journal of the Franklin Institute,* April 1894: 266–88.

*_____. *General Results of the Investigations Showing the Effect of Salicylic Acid and Salicylates Upon Digestion and Health.* Circular 31, Bureau of Agriculture, August 1906.

*_____. "Methods of Studying the Effect of Preservatives and Other Substances Added to Foods upon Health and Digestion." *Journal of the Franklin Institute,* March 1904: 161–78.

*Wiley, Harvey W. *1001 Tests of Foods, Beverages and Toilet Accessories, Good and Otherwise: Why They Are So.* Revised edition. Arranged by Anne Lewis Pierce. New York: Hearst's International Library, 1916.

*_____. "Applications of Chemistry to Public Welfare." *Journal of the Franklin Institute,* January 1911: 47–54.

*_____. *Foods and Their Adulteration: Origin, Manufacture, and Composition of Food Products; Description of Common Adulterations, Food Standards, and National Food Laws and Regulations.* Philadelphia: P. Blakiston's Son, 1907.

*_____. *Harvey W. Wiley: An Autobiography.* Indianapolis: Bobbs-Merrill, 1930.

*_____. *The History of a Crime Against the Food Law: The Amazing Story of the National Food and Drugs Law Intended to Protect the Health of the People Perverted to Protect Adulteration of Foods and Drugs.* Washington, DC: Harvey W. Wiley, M.D., 1929.

*Wiley, Harvey Washington. Papers. Manuscript Division, Library of Congress, Washington, DC.

Wilson, Bee. *Swindled: The Dark History of Food Fraud, from Poisoned Candy to Counterfeit Coffee.* Princeton, NJ: Princeton University Press, 2008.

Young, James Harvey. *American Health Quackery: Collected Essays by James Harvey Young.* Princeton, NJ: Princeton University Press, 1992.

_____. *The Medical Messiahs: A Social History of Health Quackery in Twentieth-Century America.* Princeton, NJ: Princeton University Press, 1967.

_____. *Pure Food: Securing the Federal Food and Drugs Act of 1906.* Princeton, NJ: Princeton University Press, 1989.

_____. *The Toadstool Millionaires: A Social History of Patent Medicines in America before Federal Regulation.* Princeton, NJ: Princeton University Press, 1961.

Additional articles from these sources:

American Journal of Pharmacy

American Journal of Public Health and The Nation's Health

The Analyst: The Organ of the Society of Public Analysts and Other Analytical Chemists

Bulletin of the History of Medicine

Chicago Daily Tribune

Evening Star [Washington, DC]

FDA Consumer Magazine

Forbes

Good Housekeeping

The Hill [Washington, DC]

The Independent

Journal of the American Medical Association

Journal of the History of Medicine and Allied Sciences

Ladies' Home Journal

Literary Digest

New-York Daily Tribune

New York Sun

New York Times

Public Health Reports

Smithsonian.com

Wall Street Journal

Washington Post

Washington Times

Witchita [KS] *Daily Eagle*

INDEX

Page numbers in **boldface** refer to images and/or captions.

100,000,000 Guinea Pigs, **103**, 103–104, 129

A

Accum, Fredrick, 9, 22–23
Adams, Samuel Hopkins, 57–60, **58**, **59**, 67, **68–69**
adulteration, 21, 22, 54, 67, 112, 126
    beverages, 10–12, 22, 27, 79–81
    candy, 11, 26, 28, 97, **106**, 107, 109
    food, 9–12, 20, 22–23, **23**, 25–29, **26**, 34–35, 51, 79, **89**, 113
    milk, 10, 12, 28–29, 38, **75**
alcohol, in medicine, **29**, 29–30, **53**, 56, 58, **58**, **60**, 72, 89, 111, 126
American Chamber of Horrors, 109, 129
American Medical Association (AMA), 60, 81, 96–97, 102, 109, 110, **112**
arsenic, 11, 28, 46, 126

B

bacteria, in food, 24–25, 27–28, **75**, 113, 119, 124–125, 126, 127
benzoic acid. *See* sodium benzoate
Bigelow, W. D., 43, 92
Bok, Edward, 54, 56–57, 67, **69**
borax/boric acid, **8**, 9, 27, 38, 40–44, 46, 48, 72, 90, 124
Bred Spred, 94, **94**, 107, 112–113
Brown, George Rothwell, 43–45, **44**
Bureau of Chemistry (known as Division of Chemistry pre-1901), 22, 32–33, 82, **82**, **93**, 118, 128–129, 131, 134
    drug research, 53, 57, 67, 99
    enforcement of 1906 Act, 62, 73–74, **75**, 76–77, 79–82, 90

food adulteration research, 25–28, 67, 77.
    See also Poison Squad experiments
    headquarters, **24**, **25**, **33**
    inspectors, **73**, 73–74, **75**, 77, 79, 93, **93**
    laboratories, **24**, **27**, **34**, **36**, **41**, **76**, **78**, **83**, **95**
Byers, Eben, 99–100, **100**, 107

C

Campbell, Walter, 73, **93**, 93–94, 104, 105, 110
Carter, William, **40**, **118**
Chamber of Horrors (FDA display), 105, **106**, 107–109, 129, 131
Civil War, 16–18, 23, 53, 128, **135**
coal-tar dyes, 28, 126
Coca-Cola, 79–81, **80**, **81**, 129
cocaine, **5**, **11**, **29**, 56, 58, 72, 79–80, **80**, 94, 126
codeine, 94–95, 126, 127
Collier's Weekly, 57, **57**, 59–60, **68–69**, 81, 86, 128
coloring of food, 9, 11, 26, **26**, 27–28, 32, 38, 72, **75**, 94, 112–113, 126
copper sulfate, 9, 46, **47**, 72, 76, 124
Corbett, Elizabeth Wiley (sister), 30
cosmetics, 88–89, **107**, 108
    dangerous, 96, 97, **97**, 100–104, **101**, 107, 109
    regulation of, 112–113, 118–121, **119**, 127

D

Department of Agriculture, 22, 25, 33, 86, 90, **93**, **95**, **106**, **107**, 108, 121
    Board of Food and Drug Inspection, 74, 79
    Remsen Board, 77, 79.
    See also Bureau of Chemistry;
        Campbell, Walter; Poison Squad
        experiments; Wilson, James
dial painters, **98**, 98–99, 133
Division of Chemistry. *See* Bureau
    of Chemistry

E

Elixir Sulfanilamide, 109–113, **111**, **112**, 114, 126, 129
European food bans, 29, 38, 65

F

Food and Drug Administration (FDA), **93**, 93–94, **94**, **95**, 97, 99–100, **101**, 102–104, **109**, 109–110, 112–113, 114–119, **118**, 123, **123**, 129, 131–132, 133, 134–135
    inspections, 107, 109–110, **119**, 121, 123, 132
    recalls, 110, **121**, 121–122, 123, 131
    responsibilities today, 117–123, **118**, **119**, **120**, **122**, 124–125, 126, 131.
    See also Chamber of Horrors
        (FDA display)
Food, Drug, and Cosmetic Act of 1938, 112–113, 116–117, 129, 131
Food and Drugs Act of 1906, 67, **70**, **71**, 71–72, **72**, 82, 87, 90, **91**, 92, **92**, 93, 123
    lobbying for, 29–30, 33–35, 57, 60–61, 65–67, 96, 128
    passage of, 62, 66, 128
    weaknesses, **94**, 94–97, 99–100, 102–104, **104**, 105, 107–112

food manufacturers, 12, 23–27, 32, 38, 48, 51, 61–62, 71–72, 74, 79, 82, 89, 94, 108, 119, 123, 124
    canned food, 9, 23–25, 27–28, 61, 63–64, 65, **65**, 76–77, 124–125
    factories, 9, 24–25, 73, **75**, 109, 121
    meatpacking, 62–65, **63**, **64**, **65**, **66**
formaldehyde, 10–11, 27–28, 35, 46, 72, 90, 124–125

G

General Federation of Women's Clubs, 29, 60, **85**
    state chapters, 34, 109
glucose, 10, 20, 22, 25–26, 35, 126
Good Housekeeping magazine, 82, **84**, 88–90, 92, 129, 134
Great American Fraud, The, 57, **58**, **59**

H

Hanover College, 16–18, **17**, **18**
Hapgood, Norman, 57, 67, **68–69**, 81
Harvard University, 19, 81
heroin, 72, 94, 126–127
Hostetter's Bitters, 29, **58**, 72

J

Jungle, The, 62–65, **63**, **64**, 128

K

Kefauver-Harris Amendments, 116–117, 129
Kelsey, Frances, 114–116, **117**, 133
Koremlu, 102–103, 107, 112, 127

L

Ladies' Home Journal, **56**, 56–57, 60, 128
Lakcy, Alice, 33–35, **34**, 60, 66, 79, 86, **91**
Lamb, Ruth deForest, 109, **109**
Lash Lure, 100–103, **101**, 107–108, 112, 127
lead, 11, 22, 28, 99, 126
Listerine, **103**, 104

M

McKinley, William, 32, **32**, 54, **56**, 128
Meat Inspection Amendment, 66, 128
medical devices, 96–97, **96**, 112, **118**, **119**, 120, 121, **130**, 132, **132**
morphine, 10, **10**, 53, **53**, 56, 58, 72, 94, 122, 126–127
Mrs. Winslow's Soothing Syrup, 10, **10**, 58, 72, 121
muckrakers, 67, **68–69**, 126–127, 134

N

National Consumers' League, 34, 66

O

opium, **5**, 53, 56, 58, 72, 89, 94, 126–127
Oscilloclast, 96–97, **96**

P

pharmacists, **5**, 53, 67
Poison Squad experiments, 37–51, 54, 72, 76–77, **118**, 123, 128, 134
    chemicals tested, 38, 46, 76, 124–125
    criticisms of, 48–51
    experiment setup, **40**, 40–46, **41**, 49–51, **50**, 117
    newspaper coverage, 43–46, **44, 46**, **48**, 48–49, **51**
    physical reactions, 46–50, **47**
    volunteers, **38**, 38–39, **39, 42, 43, 45**, **49**, 126

preservatives, food,
    chemical, **8**, 9–12, 25, 27–28, 37, 44–45, 90, 124–125, 126–127
    criticisms of, 27–29, 32, 48–49, 51, 72, 76, 79, 90
    current approved use, 119, 124–125
    traditional use, 27.
    See also Poison Squad experiments
Puck magazine, **5**, **23**, **53**, **66**, **68–69**
Purdue University, 19–20, 21–22, **28**
pure-food movement, 29–30, 32–35, **34**, 38, 51, 55, 56, 72, 86, 134
    opponents, 32, 54, 59–62
    supporters, 29–30, 34, 53, 60–62, 66–67. *See also* Alice Lakey

Q

quack (proprietary, patent) medicines
    and devices, 10, 18, 29–30, 52–53, **57**, 57–60, 72, **88**, 89, 93, 96, 99, **99**, 103–104, 127, 128, **130**, 132, **132**, 135
    addiction, **10**, 53, 56–58, 72
    advertising, **10**, **11**, **29**, 52, **52–53**, 56, **58**, 58–60, **59**, **60**, **80**, **81**, 95, 100, **103**, **104**, **105**
    diseases claimed to cure, **10**, **11**, 52, **52–53**, **58**, 58–59, **60**, **80**, 96, **105**.
    See also Koremlu; Lash Lure; radium

R

Radithor, 99–100, **99**, 103, 107, 113
radium, 93, **97**, 97–100, **98**, **99**, **100**, 127, 133
red clause, 59–60
Roosevelt, Eleanor, 102, 108, **108**
Roosevelt, Franklin, 105, **108**, 108–109, 112, 129
Roosevelt, Theodore, 54–56, **54–55**, 60, **65**, 65–66, 76–79, 82, 87–88, 90, 127, 128, **128**

S

saccharin, 76–77, 90, 124–125

salicylic acid, 10, 27, 46, **46**, 72, 90, 124–125

saltpeter (potassium nitrate), 27, 46, **47**, 76, 124–125

Sinclair, Upton, 62–65, **63**, **65**, **66**, 67, **69**, 96–97

sodium benzoate (benzoate of soda, benzoic acid), 27, 46, **51**, 76, 79, 90, 124

Spanish-American War, **65**, 128

sugar, 10, 20, 22, 25, 27, 55, 77, 90, 125, 126

sulfites/sulfurous acid, 46, 124–125

Sullivan, Mark, 56, 67, **69**

T

Taft, William Howard, 78–79, **79**, 82, 86–88, 129

Thacher Calculating Instrument, **50**, 131

thalidomide, 114–117, **115**, **116**, **117**, 127, 129, 133

tuberculosis, 48, 52, 59, 64, **64**, 127

U

United States Congress, 30–31, **31**, **34**, 35, 37, 54, 60, 65, 67, **70**, 74, 77, 93, 108, 109, 112, 116, 120, 128, 134

    House of Representatives, 30–31, 32, 55, 62, 66

    Senate, 30–31, 62, 66, 105

W

White House, **31**, **56**, 76–77, **85**

Wiley, Anna Kelton (wife), 80, **84–85**, 109, 129

Wiley, Harvey, 13, **22**, **23**, **24**, **28**, **30**, **33**, **36**, **43**, **55**, **70**, 71, **71**, **76**, **83**, 86, **91**, **123**, **128**, 128–129, 134–135

    childhood, **13**, 13–14, **15**, 128

    death, 92, **92**, 129

    education, 14, 16–20, **17**, **18**

    illnesses, 18, 92

    marriage and children, 80, 82, **84–85**

    professor, 19–20, 21–22

    public speaking, 17, **33**, 33–35, 51, 61, 67, **72**, 88, **89**

    resignation, 82, **86**, 86–87, **87**, **88**

    Roosevelt, Theodore (relationship with), **55**, 55–56, 76–78, 82, 87–88, 90

    soldier, **17**, 17–18, **135**.

    See also Bureau of Chemistry; Food and Drugs Act of 1906; *Good Housekeeping* magazine; Poison Squad experiments

Wiley, Lucinda (mother), 13, **14**, 16–17

Wiley, Preston (father), 13–14, **14**, 16–17

Wilson, James, 32, **32**, 55, 74, 76–77, 79–80, 82, 86, 128

Wilson, Woodrow, 88, 129

Woman's Christian Temperance Union (WCTU), **29**, 29–30, 53, 60, 108–109

PICTURE CREDITS

Samuel Hopkins Adams, *The Great American Fraud*. Chicago: Press of the American Medical Association, 1906: 58 (top and bottom), 59.

Bemidji [MN] Daily Pioneer, January 7, 1905: 44 (bottom right).

Buffalo [NY] Courier, March 16, 1912: 86.

Chicago Eagle, March 10, 1906: 64

Collier's, June 3, 1905: 57.

Country Gentleman, November 1930: 103.

Daily Press [Newport News, VA], November 23, 1906: 48.

Evening Times-Republican [Marshalltown, IA], September 17, 1903: 46 (bottom).

Film Fun, May 1922: 69 (second from bottom).

Courtesy of the **General Federation of Women's Clubs**: 34 (top).

Hyland's, hylands.com: 121.

The Independent, June 30, 1910: 81 (top).

Kalispell [MT] Bee, May 5, 1903: 137.

Ladies' Home Journal, January 1898: 56.

Library of Congress, Manuscript Division, Papers of Harvey W. Wiley: 71, 135 (top and bottom).

Library of Congress, Prints & Photographs Division:
LC-DIG-ppmsca-25463: 5; LC-USZ61-732: 17; LC-USZ61-1989: 18; LC-USZ61-733: 25; LC-USZ62-107024: 26; LC-USZ62-55447: 27; LC-USZ61-576: 30; LC-USZ61-728: 32; LC-USZ62-55763: 34 (bottom); LC-USZC2-3651: 52 (top left); LC-DIG-ppmsca-09485: 52 (bottom); LC-USZ62-5379: 54; LC-USZ61-768: 55; LC-USZ62-51782: 63 (top); LC-USZ62- 50217: 63 (bottom); LC-DIG-ppmsca-36062: 65; LC-DIG-ppmsca-26074: 66; LC-DIG-ppmsca-26036: 68-69; LC-USZ62-68363: 75 (middle left); LC-USZ62-89917: 92; LC-DIG-ppmsca-35977: 128 (top); LC-USZ62-55461: 128 (bottom); LC-USZ62-125525: 130; C. M. Bell Studio Collection: LC-B5-28192A: 22; Carol M. Highsmith Archive: LC-HS503-5903: 31(top); LC-HS503-3874: 31(bottom); George Grantham Bain Collection: LC-B2-5028-7: 69 (top); LC-B22-368-11: 69 (middle); George W. Harris Collection: LC-DIG-ppmsca-38923: 79 ; Harris & Ewing Collection: LC-H25-85182-K: 69 (second from top); LC-H261-4146: 85 (top left); LC-H22-D-1893: 107; LC-H2-B-5176-4: 108; National Photo Company Collection: LC-F81-25909: 93; LC-F82-4927: 95; New York World-Telegram and the Sun Newspaper Photograph Collection: LC-USZ62-132336: 69 (bottom); Harvey W. Wiley Collection & Papers: 13; LC-USZ6-2056: 14; 15; LC-USZ62-95796: 76; 84 (right); 85 (bottom left); 85 (right).

Los Angeles Times, October 27, 1937: 112.

Louisville [KY] Post, March 1912: 88.

Lyceum News, April 1912: 89.

National Library of Medicine, Images from the History of Medicine: front flap (top and bottom), 10, 11, 29, 43, 53 (top left and top right), 75 (top left and right), 78, 117, 118 (bottom), 119.

National Museum of Health and Medicine, Otis Historical Archives: 115.

New York Sun, October 13, 1903: 46 (top); November 11, 1908: 72.

New York Tribune, February 23, 1919: 97 (bottom right).

Perrysburg [OH] Journal, June 21, 1912: 81 (bottom).

San Francisco Call, October 12, 1903: 44 (top right).

Shutterstock, Inc.: 3, 159.

Starkville [MS] News, October 7, 1904: 60.

United States Food and Drug Administration, History Office: 23, 24, 33, 36, 38-39, 40, 41, 42, 45, 47, 49, 50, 52 (top right), 53 (bottom), 70, 73, 75 (middle right), 75 (bottom), 80, 83, 94, 96, 101, 104, 106, 111, 118 (top), 120 (top and bottom), 122, 123, 129, 132.

Courtesy of **Vassar College Library**, Archives and Special Collections, Ruth Lamb Atkinson Papers: 109.

Washington [DC] Post, April 1, 1932: 100.

Washington [Olympia] Standard, March 31, 1905: 44 (top left).

Washington [DC] Star, March 17, 1912: 87; June 13, 1924: 97 (top); October 19, 1923: 97 (left).

Washington [DC] Times, December 29, 1902: 44 (bottom left); May 21, 1904: 51.

Wellcome Collection: 8, 53 (top middle), 105, 116, 139.

Wikimedia Commons: 98; Creative Commons Attribution-Share Alike 2.0, Sam LaRussa: 99.

Harvey W. Wiley, *Harvey W. Wiley: An Autobiography*, Indianapolis: Bobbs-Merrill, 1930: 28, 84 (left), 91.

GAIL JARROW is the author of numerous nonfiction books, including *Spooked!* and her trilogy on deadly diseases: *Bubonic Panic*, *Fatal Fever*, and *Red Madness*. The most valuable lesson she has learned from studying science and history is to question assertions, analyze evidence, and dig deeper for the truth. Gail's books have received many distinctions, including a Sibert Honor, a YALSA Award Nomination for Excellence in Nonfiction, an NCSS Notable Social Studies Trade Book, the Jefferson Cup Award, and an NSTA Best STEM Book. She lives in Ithaca, New York. Visit her at gailjarrow.com.

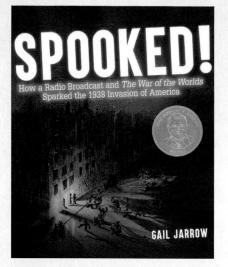

SPOOKED!:
HOW A RADIO BROADCAST AND THE WAR OF THE WORLDS SPARKED THE 1938 INVASION OF AMERICA

★ **Publishers Weekly**, starred review
★ **School Library Journal**, starred review
★ **Kirkus Reviews**, starred review
★ **Booklist**, starred review
★ **The Bulletin of the Center for Children's Books**, starred review
   A Robert F. Sibert Informational Honor Book
   An ALSC Notable Children's Book
   A **Washington Post** Best Children's Book of the Year
   A **School Library Journal** Best Book of the Year
   Booklist Editors' Choice
   A Chicago Library Best of the Best Book
   The Bulletin of the Center for Children's Books, Blue Ribbon List
   SCBWI Golden Kite Honor Book, Nonfiction for Older Readers

BUBONIC PANIC:
WHEN PLAGUE INVADED AMERICA

★ *Publishers Weekly*, starred review
★ *School Library Journal*, starred review
★ *Kirkus Reviews*, starred review
   A *Kirkus Reviews* Best Teen Book of the Year
   A *School Library Journal* Best Book of the Year
   An NSTA Outstanding Science Trade Book for Children
   An NCSS Notable Social Studies Trade Book for Children

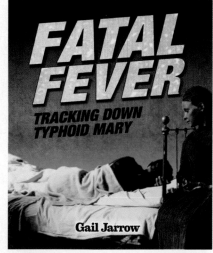

FATAL FEVER:
TRACKING DOWN TYPHOID MARY

★ *Publishers Weekly*, starred review
★ *School Library Journal*, starred review
★ *Kirkus Reviews*, starred review
★ *Booklist*, starred review
   The Bulletin of the Center for Children's Books, Blue Ribbon List
   VOYA Nonfiction Honor List
   International Literacy Association, A Best Science Book of the Year

RED MADNESS:
HOW A MEDICAL MYSTERY CHANGED WHAT WE EAT

★ *School Library Journal*, starred review
★ *Kirkus Reviews*, starred review
   A *School Library Journal* Best Book of the Year
   An NSTA Best STEM Book
   Virginia Library Association Jefferson Cup Award